Blue Paper on Data Protection

Data Transfer between the European Union and third countries:
Legal options for data controllers and data processors in a post-Brexit Britain

Guido Reinke

London – Brussels – New York

GOLD RUSH Publishing 2019

Data Transfer between the European Union and third countries:
Legal options for data controllers and data processors in a post-Brexit Britain
Copyright © 2019 GOLD RUSH Publishing®
All rights reserved.

ISBN-10: 1-90-858510-2
ISBN-13: 978-1-908585-10-3

For further information or if you wish to submit any comments or ideas for future publications, please email to the email address below.

GOLD RUSH Publishing® books may be purchased for educational, business, or sales promotional use. We are an independent publishing house promoting innovative publications.
For information please email: info@GoldRushPublishing.org.

© Guido Reinke, 2019
Data Transfer between the European Union and third countries:
Legal options for data controllers and data processors in a post-Brexit Britain
Includes text, diagrams and tables. Second Printing, edition for professionals, 2019.
978-1-908585-10-3 (ISBN 13) paperback.
Available for sale in bookshops, online at Amazon.com, and other channels worldwide.

**GOLD
RUSH**
Publishing

In the digital age
where an email and mobile phone number
are as powerful as your passport and driving license
for authenticating you as a data subject,
protecting personal data is more important than ever.

– Guido Reinke (2019)

European Data Protection is about: –

1. Empowering data subjects over their personal data

2. Consulting data subjects about collecting their personal data

3. Safeguarding and respecting the value of personal data

4. Constraining data hoarders in the age of Big Data

5. Storing and processing personal data more transparently

6. Holding data controllers and data processors more accountable

7. Transferring data only when its safety can be guaranteed

8. Obtaining consent before monetising personal data

9. Arming regulators to sanction offenders

10. Establishing a data protection ombudsman to maintain order and exercise oversight in an ever more complex data environment.

FOREWORD

by

– Lord Tim Clement-Jones CBE –
Artificial Intelligence and the necessity to manage the privacy of individuals

The UK is in a strong position to become a world leader in the development of artificial intelligence (AI). This aspiration is supported by the achievements of the UK's many leading AI companies; a dynamic academic research culture; and a robust legal, ethical, financial and linguistic framework. The Report "AI in the UK: ready, willing and able?" of the Artificial Intelligence Select Committee of the House of Lords, which I chaired, was published in April 2018. It identified some far-reaching changes that AI would bring to the UK, including boosts in productivity, further evolution of a skilled labour force, and significant impacts on social and political cohesion. It concluded that AI could deliver major improvements to the economy; however, the new capabilities will have to be managed in a responsible and ethical way.

The Report recommended the establishment of a cross-sector AI Code, with one of the five principles being a robust regime of data and privacy rights for individuals, families and communities. While the various conditions of data collection and access must be reviewed, new individual rights such as data portability should also be catered for. The UK's planned exit from the EU will add another factor to the complexity of protecting the accelerating amount of personal data generated by AI. Although the UK is committed to adhere to the GDPR, the temptation will always exist for commercial organisations, public services and intelligence agencies to go to the limits of what is possible. There is also the risk that the UK could compromise its commitment to data protection in future if pressurised by powerful stakeholders.

Safeguarding personal data processing by AI must always be a top priority. This requires putting in place adequate data transfer and data sharing agreements. This Blue Paper summarises the post-Brexit legal options that the existing EU and UK data protection frameworks provide. It offers an important contribution, advising on the lawful and ethical processing of personal data. All stakeholders having recourse to AI have a responsibility to see to it that the core principles of data protection, which includes secure data transfer, are embedded in existing and future processes and are vigorously defended.

Lord Tim Clement-Jones CBE

Lord Tim Clement-Jones CBE

Lord Clement-Jones has long experience of parliamentary affairs in the UK, in the EU, and internationally. He was Chairman of the Liberal Party from 1986 to 1988, and played a major role in its merger with the Social Democratic Party to form the Liberal Democrats. Lord Clement-Jones was made CBE for political services in 1988 and a life peer in 1998. He is now Liberal Democrat Spokesman on the Digital Economy and was Chairman of the House of Lords Select Committee on Artificial Intelligence (2017-2018) and a former member of the Select Committee on Communications (2011-2015).

FOREWORD

by

– Professor Julia Hörnle, Queen Mary University –
Data flows require trust and mutual recognition

Data is the oil of the information economy and the lynchpin for the exploitation of high-tech opportunities in data science in the 21st century. If the UK wishes to stay at the forefront of latest developments in artificial intelligence, and compete with larger countries, in particular China, innovating in this area, it needs to continue to enable international data flows in its regulatory framework.

Data flows are not binary from one country to another (say Ireland to the UK), but sequential (say from Brazil to the UK to Germany) and therefore cannot be addressed by bilateral agreements. At the same time, data flows present one of the greatest challenges for preserving human autonomy and privacy. The challenges of enabling cross-border data flows and protecting personal data at the same time cannot be solved at the national level. This is not just a question of legislation, but more importantly making regulatory decisions in response to specific issues thrown up by new technologies on an ongoing basis – this requires constant exchanges between regulatory authorities in different countries, which cannot happen ad hoc, but only within frameworks of trust and mutual recognition. It is precisely for this reason that a no-deal Brexit is so damaging to the UK economy, as well as national security and in particular cybersecurity.

International co-ordination requires mutually agreed frameworks and mechanisms within which co-ordination can take place. It is for this reason that data protection frameworks should be at the forefront of all Brexit negotiations and need to be addressed as a matter of urgency. This includes in particular the future role of the UK in the European Data Protection Board, the co-ordination body set up in the EU to deal with these issues. This is key not just for our relations with EU Member States, but equally for data flows with the rest of the world. The threat to our economy and well-being, as well as to national security are too great for this issue being thrown in the crowded pot of trade negotiation issues, which will not be resolved for many years to come.

It is precisely this dilemma of ensuring international co-ordination which this Blue

Paper addresses in a cogent and concise way, urging the UK and EU to make data protection an urgent priority. It is therefore highly recommended reading for governments and all policy-makers.

Professor Julia Hörnle

Professor Julia Hörnle, Queen Mary University of London

Julia Hörnle is a professor in Internet Law at the Centre for Commercial Law Studies, Queen Mary School of Law, University of London. She is Course Director for the LLM programme in Computer & Communications Law since 2000. Her fields of expertise are internet law and jurisdictional & regulatory issues involving the internet and she has published widely in these fields on an international level. Prof Hörnle has taught at universities in China, Germany and Austria and held a research position at Georgetown University, Washington DC, and carried out research/consultancy projects for the Chinese and UK governments and the European Commission. She is a qualified solicitor, in a former life working at Eversheds.

ACKNOWLEDGEMENTS

I am grateful to all the Chief Compliance Officers, Chief Operating officers, Chief Risk Officers, senior managers and legal counsel who have been telling me for years how complex and mystifying the legal and regulatory framework for data protection is. Politicians in the United Kingdom added another level of complexity and uncertainty by triggering Brexit without, in general, understanding the consequences, and specifically respecting the implications for cross-border data transfers. I am thankful for all these challenges, as without them there would have been no necessity for this Blue Paper.

I would like to extend my gratitude to all the professional colleagues and friends I met on the journey to writing this Paper, and the forerunners with whom I have previously published my regulatory compliance works and practitioner papers.

I am thankful to Prof. Ian Walden, Director of the Centre for Commercial Law Studies at Queen Mary University, who helped me to frame this Paper and lent focus when discussing my research at the Centre; and to Prof. Julia Hörnle, an expert on Internet law at Queen Mary University, whose criticism helped me deepen my research in crucial areas.

I could not have written this Paper without the challenges posed by my professional friends who brought their decades of experience in data protection to bear, notably Jack Nagle, Noriswadi Ismail, Thanas Loli, Fred Oberholzer, Hanna Kazerani, and Dr Klaus Meyer. I am in debt to Mikko Niva for the opportunity to gain invaluable experience in implementing GDPR for Vodafone, and to Steve Collins for entrusting me with the lead data protection role at William Hill.

Sietske de Groot and Chris MacNeil helped me sharpen my knowledge in advising SMEs in London on Brexit for the Mayor of London's office, and educating businesses that their data is a goods-like product or service that will be affected by Brexit. I am grateful too for the intellectual stimulation of Jerry W. Bains, whose legal background in particular helped me understand the multi-dimensional complexity of the legal landscape and the interference of political stakeholders.

I am grateful to Maria Balermpa at the House of Lords who gave me insight into the different mindset of Westminster politics, which does not always follow the auditor's or lawyer's logic that I am used to. After reading dozens of reports of Select Committees of the House of Lords, I acknowledge the *brain of Westminster* as superb at scrutinizing and digesting the Government's and Commons' work. I am grateful in particular to Lord Tim Clement-Jones for sharing his understanding with me and writing a foreword to this paper.

My MP, Jim Fitzpatrick, too, must no go unacknowledged, who graced me with a private tour of Westminster Palace and who introduced me to the Digital, Culture, Media and Sport Select Committee of the House of Commons, which is preparing the foundation work concerning data protection post-Brexit.

Above all, I am thankful for my friends and family who have supported and encouraged me, particular in dark moments when I feared I was drowning in the deluge of Brexit. My parents provided me endless inspiration on this topic, how cookies and privacy notices affect their lives. This Blue Paper is dedicated to them, and to all who have supported me in this endeavour, and who have given me their advice, but more importantly, their enthusiasm.

Guido Reinke

TABLE OF CONTENTS

LIST OF ACRONYMS

AI	Artificial Intelligence
APEC	Asia-Pacific Economic Cooperation
APPI	Act on the Protection of Personal Information (Japan)
Art. 29 WP	Article 29 Working Party
BCRs	Binding Corporate Rules
Brexit	Britain's Exit from the EU
CBI	Confederation of British Industry
CETA	Comprehensive Economic Trade Agreement
CETS	Council of Europe Treaty Series
CFR	EU Charter of Fundamental Rights
CoE	Council of Europe
DeExEU	Department for Exiting the European Union
ECHR	European Convention on Human Rights
ECtHR	European Court on Human Rights
EDPB	European Data Protection Board
EEA	European Economic Area
ETS	European Treaty Series
CJEU	Court of Justice of the European Union, in the literature also referred to as the European Court of Justice (ECJ)
GDPR	General Data Protection Regulation
ICC	International Chamber of Commerce
ICO	Information Commissioner's Office (UK)
IPCO	Investigatory Powers Commissioner's Office
NSA	National Security Agency (USA)
OECD	Organisation for Economic Co-operation and Development
PPC	Personal Information Protection Commission (Japan)
PECA	Privacy and Electronic Communications Act
SMEs	Small and medium-sized enterprises
SCCs	Standard Contract Clauses (or "model [contract] clauses")
UNESCO	United Nations Educational, Scientific and Cultural Organization

UNCTAD	United Nations Conference on Trade and Development
WTO	World Trade Organization

EXECUTIVE SUMMARY

The law of the European Single Market (or Internal Market), laid out in the Treaty of Rome, guarantees "four freedoms" within the European Union: the free movement of goods, services, capital, and labour. The transition to a digital economy and the increasing importance of (personal) Big Data ought to suggest recognition of a fifth freedom: *the free movement of data.*

1. Assessment of legal options

The UK economy is data-driven; its success depends on the untrammelled cross-border movement of data. However, data moving between the EU and the UK post-Brexit must be processed and transferred within the adequate legal framework decreed by the EU. The two parties ought therefore to give the highest priority to getting the UK's post-Brexit legal framework recognised by the European Commission as adequate, and to working out a data protection agreement. The objectives of any common legal framework must be clearly defined and include regulatory cooperation that goes beyond mere recognition which the Commission's data adequacy decision provides. Ideally, it ought to give the ICO (the UK data regulator) a seat as an observer on the European Data Protection Board (EDPB), and on that basis allow its ongoing participation in the "one-stop shop" mechanism, and to empower the ICO to approve codes of conduct and certifications if issued under the GDPR. This would benefit not only UK but also EU businesses and citizens.

Prospective third-country trading partners of the UK are likely to continue to be assessed by the European Commission as "inadequate" under EU data protection standards. Yet the UK may none the less need trade agreements with such countries. The EDPB can help the UK negotiate alternative protection mechanisms substituting for an EU adequacy decision.

The EU (Withdrawal) Act 2018 enshrines the EU's General Data Protection Regulation (GDPR) in UK statute law, so that its fundamental principles, the obligations it imposes on business organisations, and the rights it accords to data subjects will continue to stand. Notwithstanding this milestone, uncertainty persists as at October 2019 concerning data-transfers between the EU and the UK, and access to EU databases from the UK in the immediate future, due to lack of an actual decision on the adequacy of the UK's post-Brexit data protection regime. Although Committees of the House of Lords, House of Commons, and European Commission have identified key issues, no specific action has been taken. This is also due to the Commission's insistence that the UK must leave the EU before it will take any decision. There are only two realistic scenarios on the day after Brexit concerning the flow of data between the EU and the UK:

(1)　the UK leaves the EU on terms negotiated in a withdrawal agreement, enabling businesses to adjust their data processing accordingly during any transition period; or else

(2)　the UK leaves the EU with No-deal, thus becoming an ordinary "third country" with immediate effect, imposing more bureaucratic procedures and costs on businesses.

This Blue Paper focusses on data transfers between the EU/EEA and the UK. The UK Government stated in its *No-deal Guidance* that it will "transitionally recognise all EEA states, EU and EEA institutions and Gibraltar as providing an adequate level of protection for personal data. This means that personal data can continue to flow freely from the UK to these destinations following the UK's exit from the EU" (HM Government, 23 April 2019). But the flow of data in the other direction – into the UK from those countries – might be interrupted.

2.　Policy Recommendations

Based on analysis of the legal options available post-Brexit for EU-to-UK data transfers, the following conclusions about best practice and sound policy in data protection may be drawn:

(1)　The UK should initiate as soon as possible the process for an adequacy assessment by the European Commission. As noted above, the UK Government has already given unilateral approval of data transfers from the UK to the EU.

(2)　If at all possible, a special transitional personal data arrangement identical to Articles 70 to 74 of the Withdrawal Agreement should be negotiated immediately in order to safeguard e-commerce and avoid a data-interruption "cliff-edge" in the eventuality of a No-deal Brexit. Such a special arrangement would also provide for uninterrupted data flow in case, after the transition period ends, a formal adequacy decision has not been made by the European Commission or a mutual data agreement between both jurisdictions has not been agreed.

(3)　The UK should not take an EU adequacy decision for granted merely because it has enacted the GDPR into UK statutory law and has established a recognised independent regulatory authority for data protection. It should listen to the concerns of civil right groups and comments from EU representatives, and implement measures to either remediate concerns about its data protection framework, or at least mitigate them. Recommendations for addressing key concerns are as follows. The UK should –

(a)   continue its membership of the European Convention on Human Rights, including the jurisdiction of the European Court of Human Rights and adhering to its judgements on human right issues; especially continuing to enforce Article 8 of the European Convention on Human Rights; and

(b)   continue to adhere to the Council of Europe's Convention for the Protection of Individuals with regard to Automatic Processing of Personal Data 1981, ETS No. 108.

(c)   bear in mind that Brexit means irrevocable exit from the EU Charter of Fundamental Rights.

(d)   review its own legal framework, and in particular: the Investigatory Powers Act (IPA) 2016, the extraordinary powers which the intelligence services are already using, and the exceptions for immigration services in the Data Protection Act 2018. The EU will closely monitor how the Home Office reviews settled status applications for EU citizens post-Brexit, and whether data subjects can obtain full access to their personal data in disputes.

(e)   revise its practices in handling personal data for national security purposes, in particular individual and mass surveillance practices, data retention schedules, and data sharing arrangements under the Five Eyes agreement.

(4)   The UK must develop its own regime similar to the EU's adequacy framework to assure that personal data transfers to third countries outside the EU are protected in line with the principles of the GDPR. It either can continue to rely on the EU's adequacy decisions or ignore these and create its own assessment procedures, which will be needed anyway if the UK plans to include data transfer in its trade agreements with countries outside the EU.

(5)   The ICO should work with business to develop new Standard Contractual Clauses to assist in case of an EU no-adequacy decision or no EU-UK data protection agreement. The only two model clauses that exist to date are for EU Controller to non-EU Controller and EU Controller to non-EU Processor. A model clause for EU Processor to non-EU Sub-Processor (and *vice versa*), for example, would be desirable.

(6)   Parliament should assess the wider implications of Brexit for data flows; in particular, it should instruct its committees to:

(a)   assess the needs of the several business sectors, especially those highly dependent on continuous free data flows, Big Data, and data analytics: retailers, financial services, international transport, and the travel industry. Early engagement with stakeholders is recommended to help shape an EU-UK data agreement, which could consist of sector-specific agreements if the EU rejects a generic one.

(b) identify which non-personal data flows might be interrupted by Brexit. The "Free Flow Regulation", adopted on 14 November 2018 (Regulation (EU) 2018/1807, 14 November 2018) establishes the same principles for the free movement of non-personal data within the EU as did Regulation EU 2016/679 for personal data.

(c) define the role of the CJEU in the case of data transfers and possible data breaches of EU-citizen personal data in the UK. When the UK leaves the EU, the jurisdiction of the CJEU over the UK will end as well; however, as the European Data Protection Supervisor has the power to refer a matter to the CJEU, and many data protection cases have an international dimension, the UK should consider adhering to CJEU judgments voluntarily as a matter of policy, or enacting a special conflict-of-laws mechanism (*e.g.* for dispute resolution) to address this.

(d) explore the implications of non-business data exchanges and what might happen in case the UK was locked out of EU law enforcement databases after Brexit. This should cover data exchange/access for:

(i) law enforcement, for example, to the European Arrest Warrant (EAW) Information System;

(ii) national security agencies and border control to the Schengen Information System (SIS II), the European Criminal Records Information System (ECRIS), the European Asylum Dactyloscopy Database (Eurodac), and the Prüm Framework (DNA and fingerprint database);

(iii) specialised agencies fighting against terrorism, cybercrime and other serious forms of organised crime to Europol and EU Justice and Home Affairs databases.

3. Overview of legal options for data transfer post-Brexit

The following table provides an overview of the legal options covering transfers of personal data between the EU and UK that are examined in this Blue Paper. It is assumed that the UK will not in future enact any legislation affecting these options which the EU would not be willing to live with. The suitability of these options should be assessed on a case-by-case basis. Organisational preferences and the decision of which legal options to choose will depend on many variables, such as:

- organisational size (small and medium-sized organisations *vs.* multinational organisations), structure (*e.g.* international organisations with internal data centres vs. outsourcing to a third-party provider), and core business activities (*e.g.* health care provider vs. manufacturing industry);
- risk appetite as determined by likelihood and impact of detrimental data incidents;
- sensitivity of the personal data processed: Article 9(1) prohibition on processing "special categories of data" (*e.g.* data revealing a natural person's racial or ethnic origin) *vs.* systematic monitoring of a publicly accessible area (*e.g.* CCTV feed) requiring only an internal impact assessment;
- risk of processing; *e.g.* automated analytical mass profiling *vs.* manual processing system targeting individual data subjects; and
- ambit of data flows to third parties with processor and sub-processor responsibilities; *e.g.* external marketing company outsourcing campaign to direct-mail specialist *vs.* personal data processed only in house by internal marketing department.

Figure 1: Legal options for data transfer between the EU and UK (post-Brexit)

Note: All Articles in this table refer to the General Data Protection Regulation

Option 1: Partial or full adequacy decision (Article 45) *Preferability: High*	
Scope	For a third country to transfer personal data to itself from the EU27 or EEA (Norway, Iceland and Liechtenstein)/EFTA (plus Switzerland) countries. Adequacy decisions are reviewed once every four years at the latest.
Practicability for businesses	No additional effort is required for businesses. Partial adequacy decisions such as the Privacy Shield (USA) or Personal Info Protection Act 2000 (Canada) exclude specific sectors (*e.g.* financial services and insurance sector, public services).
Availability to the UK market	Can only be granted by the European Commission (UK decision expected no sooner than 31 Dec 2020). Article 45(2) and Recital 104 set out the list of criteria for an adequate level of protection. If only sector-specific arrangements (like the Privacy Shield) can be achieved, then the decision will not cover all industries. Available to all organisations in the UK if the decision is for full adequacy. The third country, territory, or one or more specified sectors within either, or the international organisation in question are deemed to have an adequate level of protection (Article 45(2)). So far, only thirteen third countries have been deemed to provide adequate protection under Article 45 (the so called "white list"). Adequacy for the free data flows has become an important item for negotiation in trade agreements. The white list includes Andorra, Argentina, Canada (commercial organisations), Faroe Islands, Guernsey, Israel, Isle of Man, Japan, Jersey, New Zealand, Switzerland, Uruguay, and the USA (Privacy Shield framework) as providing adequate protection.
Brexit implications	The UK's preferred option is to obtain a full adequacy decision. If this does not happen, alternative options are presented below, which must be implemented.

Option 2: Standard Contractual Clauses (Article 46(2)(c)) Also known as Standard data protection clauses, service contracts, or data processing agreements. *Preferability: Medium*	
Scope	European Commission has adopted two sets of model clauses for data transfer to (non-EU) third countries, namely: (1) EU Controller to non-EU or EEA Controller, and (2) EU Controller to non-EU or EEA Processor.
Practicability for businesses	Depending on the data flow, this can entail excessive legal paperwork. This mechanism must have strong legal input to add the data protection clauses to the master contract. Scale of implementation depends on the organisation's structural complexity. At a minimum, the SCC must include: (1) the data processor "processes the personal data only on documented instructions from the controller"; and (2) the processor has "sufficient guarantees to implement appropriate technical and organisational measures" (Article 28(1)) to prevent unauthorised or unlawful processing of, and accidental loss or damage of personal data.
Availability to the UK market	In the absence of an EU adequacy decision, standard contractual clauses may substitute as a mechanism to ensure adequacy by the contractual parties (only). SCCs may be adopted by the European Commission (Article 46(2)(c)) or by Member States' Supervisory Authorities and then approved by the Commission (Article 46(2)(d)). Before a data processor carries out any processing on behalf of a data controller, the latter must have a prior specific or general written authorisation between the two parties (Article 28).
Brexit implications	The UK government have recognised existing EU SSCs, but future SCCs issued by the UK Regulator yet not adopted by the European Commission may cover data transfers from the UK to the EU, but will not cover transfers the other way, from the EU to the UK. It remains a question whether the UK will adopt EU adequacy decisions in future, and whether it will rely on the same adequacy decisions by third countries as the EU will do.

Option 3: Binding Corporate Rules (Articles 46(2)(b) and 47) *Preferability: Low (likely to be inapplicable)*	
Scope	BCRs govern personal data transfers between EU and overseas divisions of corporate groups (including franchises) and inside other international organisations.
Practicability for businesses	The process is complex, lengthy (12 months+) and costly (£250,000 to set up on average), requiring strong legal input and close collaboration with the European Commission. This option is not designed for the "mass market": as at 25 May 2018 only 131 EU companies had obtained authorisations from the EU, including 27 from the UK's ICO.
Availability to the UK market	Approval by the European Commission is required.
Brexit implications	Post-Brexit, the ICO will not partake in the BCR community. BCRs will be no viable option for UK companies transferring data from the EU to the UK. The EDPB published a No-deal Brexit Information Note for organisations that have already selected the ICO as the BCR Lead Supervisory Authority, clearly stating that the ICO can no longer supervise BCRs.

Option 4a: Approved Codes of conduct (Article 46(2)(e), Articles 40-41)	
Preferability: Medium (dependent on contract)	
Scope	This mechanism contains binding commitments to EU data subjects by third-country organisations.
Practicability for businesses	This new instrument helps meet both data transfer obligations in specific sectors and the needs of micro-companies and SMEs. Committing to a code of conduct is voluntary, but can demonstrate the organisation follows best practice. All Codes of conduct must contain procedures for effectively monitoring code compliance through accredited and independent bodies.
Availability to the UK market	The EDPB defines the process for committing to Codes of conduct, acceptance criteria for codes, and requirements for issuing bodies (EDPB, 4 June 2019 [Guidelines 1/2019]). The competent Supervisory Authority must provide an opinion on whether a code of conduct complies with the GDPR, then approve the draft code (Article 40(5)). The Commission, after due examination, may decide to adopt a code recommended by the EDPB as having general validity within the EU, then make the code publicly available (Article 40(8-11)). The Supervisory Authority must also accredit independent code-issuing bodies and is responsible for monitoring compliance with the code (Article 41(1)).
Brexit implications	It is unclear what role the UK's ICO will play post-Brexit in the EU's process of accepting national (let alone transnational) codes. Will there be a "special relationship" between the UK's ICO and the EU's EDPB? Can the ICO's Codes of conduct be published in the EDPB's public register? Nor will future codes issued under the EDPB or the European Commission automatically apply in the UK without ICO approval. Other issues include whether EU cooperation will be forthcoming if a transnational code of conduct has identified the UK's ICO as the Competent Supervisory Authority in monitoring and enforcing the code.

Option 4b: Data protection certifications, marks and seals (Article 46(2)(f), Articles 42-43)	
Preferability: Medium (dependent on contract)	
Scope	This mechanism contains binding commitments to EU data subjects by third-country organisations. Certifications support transfers of EU personal data to third countries or international organisations (Article 46(2)(f)).
Practicability for businesses	This should in particular assist specific requirements in various sectors and the needs of micro-companies and SMEs. Certifications, seals and marks are voluntary schemes to evidence that accountability principles proffered by the controller and processor actually safeguard personal data. Additional binding commitments via contractual or other legally binding instruments are expected (Article 42(2)).
Availability to the UK market	The EDPB defines the process of accrediting certification bodies. It may also adopt the "European Data Protection Seal" (Article 42(5)), a certification in common. The competent Supervisory Authority or the EDPB issues the certification which lasts no more than three years, is subject to periodic reviews, and then comes up for renewal. The Supervisory Authorities must also accredit independent certification bodies to handle the issuance, periodic review, and withdrawal of certifications (Article 43).
Brexit implications	The UK will lose its influence on the EDPB in issuing certifications, exercising oversight, and choosing which certification schemes, seals and marks to include in the EU register; as well as over any future European Data Protection Seal. And will the UK comply with EU technical standards for the certification procedures, seals and marks according to EU law, to make them applicable inside the UK?

Option 5: Derogations, including consent, contract performance, or legitimate interest (Article 49) *Preferability: Medium (limited applicability)*	
Scope	Derogations from GDPR in specified situations as a basis for exceptional personal data transfers should be but occasional, affect a limited number of data subjects, and be necessary to, without compromising subjects' compelling legitimate interests and rights.
Practicability for businesses	Organisations resort to derogations of the following categories: (1) Explicit consent by the data subject (Art. 49(1)(a)) (2) Necessity for contractual performance (Art. 49(1)(b)) (3) Legitimate interest amongst other reasons (Art. 49(1)(c-g)). On the conditions set by Article 49(1), derogations are an option for transferring personal data even to third countries lacking an adequacy decision from the EU.
Availability to the UK market	Special circumstances apply that allow to resort to derogations. In case of non-adequacy decision or lack of appropriate safeguards, transfers of personal data to a third country or an international organisation may take place under the terms and conditions of Article 49 relating to exceptional circumstances.
Brexit implications	Not applicable (assuming the UK legislates no derogations of its own which the EU would not accept).

Option 6: Transitional agreement on personal data *Preferability: High (temporary and one-off)*	
Scope	A special transitional arrangement identical to Articles 70-74 of the Withdrawal Agreement could be negotiated.
Practicability for businesses	Businesses may lobby for this. A "cliff edge" scenario that finds the UK non-adequate would impose bureaucratic costs on businesses.
Brexit implications	It mitigates the risk of a "limbo" between the EU and UK with no data transfer agreement in place (in a transition period or No-deal scenario), to safeguard e-commerce and avoid a data-interruption "cliff edge". Such a special arrangement would also provide for uninterrupted data flow in case, after the transition period, a formal adequacy decision has not been made by the European Commission, or a mutual data agreement between EU and UK has not been agreed.

Option 7: New EU-UK data protection agreement (UK specific)	
Preferability: High (if unlikely)	
Scope	The current vision of an international data treaty is to utilise the existing adequacy model and empower a UK regulator to closely collaborate with the EDPB.
Practicability for businesses	Businesses may lobby for this, but have limited influence apart from expressing interest in continued use of existing mechanisms in the UK, such as BCRs, Codes of conduct and certifications. Continuation of ICO's membership of the EDPB and participation in the EU's "one-stop shop" would reduce costs and red tape for businesses by letting them deal with just one data protection authority.
Brexit implications	The "technical note" published by the UK Government (June 2018) and the more detailed White Paper "The exchange and protection of personal data – a future partnership paper" (24 August 2018) outline the scope of such an agreement. The new agreement should provide robust safeguards, allow the UK to work alongside the EU and other international partners to boost data protection standards, and forge a strong partnership that builds on the existing adequacy model. This requires close and effective cooperation between the ICO and EU regulators.

PART I

Possible Post-Brexit Data Transfer Solutions

Historically, privacy was almost implicit, because it was hard to find and gather information.
But in the digital world, whether it's digital cameras or satellites or just what you click on, we need to have more explicit rules – not just for governments but for private companies.

– Bill Gates

Chapter 1

INTRODUCTION

1.1 The importance of the free flow of data in today's digital economy

It is widely acknowledged that in today's digital economy personal data is the *new oil* (Sunday Independent, 2018). Thus, Josh Hardie, Deputy Director-General of Confederation of British Industry (CBI) stressed the importance of reaching agreement rapidly on data exchange with the EU to protect the UK's data-driven businesses and the £240 billion they contribute to the UK economy (Price, 2017). It is also the reason why Kuner, after researching the multi-dimensional aspects (economic, political and social) of transborder data flows and having created an inventory of regulations at a global level, called for a reflection about its aims, operation, and effectiveness. He criticised especially the lack of transparency on transborder data flow regulation and how this constrains individuals' power to assert their rights over cross-border data transfers of their own very personal matters (Kuner, 2010).

The EU has been putting safeguard agreements on cross-border data transfers into its international trade deals, as evidenced by all the critics who have been complaining that that these codicils mandate a form of protectionism to retain and process data locally (*i.e.* in the EU) (Beattie, 2017), but privacy advocates resist the proliferation of unconsented surveillance. Not surprisingly, the UK Government and regulator are already committed to align the UK data protection regime as closely as possible with the EU, post-Brexit (Financial Times, 2018). Allie Renison, head of EU and trade policy at the Institute of Directors, expects that the UK's "deep integration with the EU on data flows should make reaching a short-term agreement easier to negotiate"; however, Renison is prioritising an adequacy assessment for the interim period over a complex "unique model", which should be the long term ambition (Stone, 2017). Most of the white papers drawn up by the UK Government, parliamentary committees, and independent researchers recognise the importance of (personal) data; however, no one has done a detailed analysis of the different legal options organisations have for transferring data from the EU to the UK post-Brexit.

The present Blue Paper aims to fill this gap by critically reviewing the options in the existing legal framework and in the new political and legal realities of post-Brexit Britain.

1.2   Key objectives, assumptions and value for data controllers

The objective of this empirically oriented Blue Paper[1] is to critically analyse the various legal options for transfer of personal data to the UK from the European Union (EU) and/or the European Economic Area (EEA) that can be made available to organisations operating from a "third country". The transfer of personal data from the UK to the EU seems to be less an issue, even in the case of a No-deal Brexit, as the UK government intends to impose no restrictions on data transfers to the EU or EEA. The UK Government's No-deal Guidance for Data "transitionally recognises all EEA countries (including EU Member States) and Gibraltar as 'adequate' to allow data flows from the UK to Europe to continue" (HM Government, 23 April 2019); however, the UK will conserve the extraterritorial scope of data protection law, like EU Member States, and the existing EU adequacy decisions on a transitional basis (HM Government, 23 April 2019). This Paper, however, is not concerned with the transition period, which would maintain the *status quo*, but with the point when the UK formally leaves the EU and becomes a third country. The assumption herein is that the country where the data controller has its main establishment (the UK) is an EU Member State in process of seceding, and becomes a third country on the exit date. To illustrate these options, the author will use the most stressful, worst-case Brexit scenario (the exit of the United Kingdom from the EU), that is, a hard or No-deal Brexit, with the UK considered as an exceptional case among "third countries" – which generally seek to set up a data transfer regime from scratch. The UK has been part of the EU's data transfer regime from the beginning, but is now seeking a special relationship with the EU amid exiting it.

This unique event deserves further examination considering the financial investments and resource efforts that UK businesses and the Regulator have undertaken to achieve full compliance with the General Data Protection Regulation (GDPR). When the UK leaves the EU, organisations based in the UK will have to process personal data in line with the GDPR requirements. Due to the importance of personal data for business operations, marketing and sales, and other valuable purposes, Brexit has put and will continue to put a spotlight on the regulatory framework for safeguarding the processing and transfer of personal data. At

---

[1]   A "Blue Paper" is neither a *White Paper*, an official government report giving information or proposals on an issue, nor a *Green Paper*, a preliminary UK Government or EU proposal that has been published in order to stimulate debate. I am introducing the novel term *Blue Paper* to designate an analysis and guidance paper that reviews the *legal options*, in this case for data transfers post-Brexit. The content of a Blue Paper, however, is not theoretical nor pitched to lawyers, but to the laity. It strikes a practical balance for professionals working across functions, giving them a robust range of options if personal data has to be transferred by HR, marketing, sales and other functions.

the time of writing this Blue Paper, the United Kingdom had not passed any law nor ratified any agreement with the EU defining its legal position post-Brexit. The scope only addresses the options between "third countries" and the EU, the political debate about different scenarios of the future relationship between the UK and EU, such as staying in the Customs Union, or a Norway-style or Canada-plus arrangement, can be ignored. In case of a no-Brexit scenario, valuable lessons can be still learned from this Brexit case study.

It is assumed that the UK will leave the Single Market and that it will officially become a third country when the UK exits the EU either without a deal ("hard Brexit") and without a transition period, or else on 31 December 2020 at the end of the transition period (or later) as defined in the Draft Withdrawal Agreement of 14 Nov 2018. It is also assumed that any new instrument allowing data transfer will be based on existing instruments; it might be a combination thereof or require some involvement of regulatory authorities or other bodies.

1.3   Scope of the Blue Paper

As the Brexit process is ongoing and it could take up to three years to settle with the EU the UK's position respecting data transfer, this paper will review the standard legal options already available through the GDPR and other legal texts. It will also critically analyse the "ambitious" legal options referred-to in official documents of the UK government. This paper will not engage in a political debate, but will focus solely on mechanisms that would help UK-based companies to be compliant by meeting the legal and regulatory requirements of UK and EU law. The objective is to take up a lawyer's standpoint to help organisations minimise liability when transferring personal data.

The ultimate objective of this Blue Paper is to assist affected organisations to achieve compliance based on the legal options available. Organisations have different structures, different levels of complexity of internal and third-party data processors, and are processing different types of personal data, depending on the nature of their activities (*e.g.* employee data, customer data, sensitive data, and/or high volumes of data); therefore, there is no one-size-fits-all solution, and so each organisation ought to assess which legal option(s) fit the best for them.

1.4   Structure of this Paper

Chapter One provides some background on the topic of this Blue Paper, and defines its objectives, basic assumptions, and scope.

Chapter Two gives an overview of the legal sources to be relied on, and reviews key

Brexit-related documents which explain the UK's position on data protection and data transfer. It also presents the legal instruments that are available for data transfers, and the dilemma that the UK faces in making its own free trade agreements with third countries.

Chapter Three analyse the solutions offered for data transfer between the EU and those third countries deemed adequate. It reviews the thirteen adequacy decisions granted by the European Commission to date, looking in particular at the criteria on which the decision was based. It also briefly compares adequacy versus partial and non-adequacy decisions, and provides some insights into the EU-US Safe Harbour Principles and Privacy Shield. The mutual EU-Japan agreement is also analysed, the only adequacy decision taken under GDPR so far. The chapter also explores the UK's international data flows outside the EU, and the EU-adequacy implications of future trade agreements with third countries. It concludes with an assessment of the likelihood of a non-adequacy decision for the UK.

Chapter Four reviews the *toolkits* available to organisations in the absence of an adequacy decision. These include Standard Contract Clauses (SCCs), Codes of Conduct, and certification by accredited third parties. Also to be explained is why Binding Corporate Rules (BCRs) are not an viable post-Brexit option, nor the derogations from the rules for specific purposes.

Chapter Five investigates which other legal options may become available. The UK Brexit negotiators expressed interest in a new form of agreement in a "Technical Note: Benefits of a new data protection agreement between the EU and the UK" (DExEU, 7 June 2018) and in the "Political Declaration setting out the framework for the future relationship between the European Union and the United Kingdom" (DExEU, 25 Nov 2018). This Chapter also provides further analysis of an approach to negotiating a new EU-UK agreement for data protection using the UK's sophisticated intelligence and security capabilities as bargaining chips.

Chapter Six is an analysis of law enforcement data handling and special data provisions for national security. This is a extraordinary topic and could make up a Blue Paper in itself. It would have to include the Investigatory Powers Act (IPA) of 2016, – special powers given to intelligence services to access personal data, – as well as the exceptions for the immigration enforcement services in the Data Protection Act 2018. It would also cover individual and mass surveillance practices, data retention schedules, and data sharing arrangements under the Five Eyes agreement. For purposes of this Paper, the only relevance of law enforcement and national security data processing is if the UK were to use the valuable yield of it as a "bargaining chip" in negotiating a special relationship data transfer agreement. Yet the European Commission could make an issue of the practices of the same UK intelligence services when assessing the UK under its adequacy requirements, hence this may inure to the advantage of either negotiating party.

The final part, Chapter Seven and the Executive Summary, critically analyses all known legal options available to assess which ones may be preferable from the standpoint of risk both legal (*i.e.* liability) and commercial (*i.e.* costs and time), and concludes by making policy recommendations.   The overarching objective is rigorously to overview how the interests of organisations, data subjects, and regulators might be accommodated in a balanced way. The summary gives a final snapshot of the topic.

The Executive Summary provides a simple checklist titled "Overview – Legal options for data transfer post-Brexit" to help organisations gauge the best legal options for themselves. It summarizes for each legal option its scope, its practicability for businesses and availability to the UK market, and its Brexit implications.

To help identify and assess the value of the several legal options, each of Chapters Two through Four will cover, firstly, a brief overview of the options with reference to key legal sources, and secondly, a rigorous comparative analysis of the advantages and disadvantages of each option. This includes their applicability to a post-Brexit UK and an evaluation of the impact of Brexit thereon. In conclusion, this Blue Paper offers a perspective that will be useful for the UK as a country and for businesses operating within the UK who need to transfer personal data to and from the EU. Finally, some conjectural implications are brought up for discussion.

Chapter 2

THE UK'S DATA TRANSFER PROBLEM AND POSSIBLE SOLUTIONS

2.1 The UK's post-Brexit data transfer challenge

This chapter outlines the challenges that post-Brexit Britain faces, especially if no Withdrawal Agreement or no alternative *modus vivendi* between the EU and UK is agreed (*i.e.* the Hard Brexit case). The UK will exit the Court of Justice of the European Union's (CJEU's) jurisdiction, meaning that the EU will no longer be able to enforce the GDPR in the UK. The European Court of Human Rights (ECtHR), to whose jurisdiction the UK remains subject post-Brexit under the European Convention on Human Rights (ECHR), has made some landmark privacy and data protection rulings: on abuse of state eavesdropping powers (*Case of Klass and others v. Germany*); mass surveillance (*Big Brother Watch and others v. the UK*); interception of telephone conversations (*Malone v. United Kingdom*); blanket mobile phone interception devices (*Case of Roman Zakharov v. Russia*); excessive collection of medical data (*Case of L.H. v. Latvia*).[2] As these recent cases involving the UK show, data protection and privacy is a key concern of civil liberties groups, but also of the European Commission. These rulings, important thought they are, have not sufficed to quiet all of the Commission's concerns about the privacy of data being transferred from the EU to the UK, because of the ongoing conflict with existing law enforcement and surveillance practices in the UK. Moreover, the ECtHR jurisprudence has not been able to cover the gamut of data transfer issues due to the ECHR's unspecificity about data processing. This introduces an element of doubt about the long-term equivalence of UK and EU data privacy and protection law. Arguably, this state of legal affairs is suspect as putting the UK in a weak position to maintain in the long run its post-Brexit data privacy adequacy under EU law, as circumstances change and Governments come and go (*e.g.*, the Withdrawal Agreement negotiated by the May Government which was rejected first thing by the new Government

---

[2]   Further European Court of Human Rights cases can be reviewed on the ECHR database, which is available at https://hudoc.echr.coe.int.

of Boris Johnson of the same political party). The Brexiters speak of "taking back control of the laws" by leaving the jurisdiction of the European Court of Justice (EJC). Given the pressure the UK is under to replace EU trade agreements with its own, this autonomy may be a double-edged sword if it complicates the process of aligning the UK with the EU's adequacy criteria in protecting the personal data of EU citizens. It is thought best to stabilise the UK data regime by incorporating it in an international (*viz.* supra-UK) legal regime. After assessing Convention 108, a multilateral treaty drafted by the Council of Europe, the author argues that this is the best instrument for helping the UK over this disadvantage.

2.2   The current privacy framework

2.2.1   GDPR and the UK Data Protection Act 2018

The General Data Protection Regulation (GDPR) – Regulation (EU) 2016/679 of the European Parliament and of the Council of 27 April 2016 on "the protection of natural persons with regard to the processing of personal data and on the free movement of such data, and repealing Directive 95/46/EC" – strengthens the previous EU data protection framework, which was embodied under Directive 95/46/EC of the European Parliament and the Council of 24 October 1995 on "the protection of individuals with regard to the processing of personal data and on the free movement of such data". The GDPR sets stricter standards sets in regards to territorial scope and data transfer. In the context of EU data protection regulation, this has been rather an evolution than a revolution.

Article 3 of the GDPR states that it "applies to the processing of personal data in the context of the activities of an establishment of a controller or a processor in the Union, regardless of whether the processing takes place in the Union or not." Like the Council of Europe, GDPR introduced seven principles (lawfulness, fairness and transparency; purpose limitation; data minimisation; accuracy; storage limitation; integrity and confidentiality; accountability) which provide a baseline and indirect political aim to be globally adopted.

Kuner has noted that GDPR introduced a number of major changes to the EU regulatory framework on data transfer. Article 46 abandons the presumption under Directive 95/46/EC that personal data may not be transferred if there is no "adequacy level of protection in the recipient country". As long as all provisions of the GDPR are met, transfers are possible. The three mechanisms that allow transfers are a Commission's adequacy decision (Article 45); the use of "appropriate safeguards" (Article 46, including Binding Corporate Rules under Article 47); or certain enumerated derogations (Article 49). Article 45(1) makes adequacy decision-making more flexible by widening the scope beyond countries to include "territories" or "specified sectors" within a third country or international organisation (Kuner, 2013:46-47). Article 50 encourages the Commission and Member States' Supervisory Authorities to cooperate internationally for the protection of personal data, recommending specific steps.

The GDPR was transposed by the Data Protection Act 2018 and since 23 May has been UK law. The UK's Data Protection Act 2018 ch. 12, which replaced the Data Protection Act 1998 ch. 29, aims to empower data subjects to take more control of their data in the digital age. It features provisions governing the processing of personal data, including novelties such as mandatory data breach notification, increased penalties, "the right to be forgotten", and the concept of privacy by design. It transposes the General Data Protection Regulation (EU 2016/679), which aspires to the ideal of individual empowerment. The UK will be fully aligned with the EU data protection regime after Brexit, Deal or No-deal.

Actually, the Data Protection Act 2018 transposes not only the GDPR, but also the Data Protection Law Enforcement Directive (EU 2016/680), which protects civil rights when personal data is collected by government authorities for law enforcement purposes and for national security. It provides for derogations in the areas of academic research, financial services, and child protection (HM Government, 23 May 2018).

2.2.2   EU Charter of Fundamental Rights

The EU Charter of Fundamental Rights (CFR) (European Union, 2000), which is patterned after the ECHR, the European Social Charter, and other EU law, enumerates and enacts to the benefit of the peoples of Europe certain substantive rights to dignity, freedoms, equality, solidarity, citizenship and justice, to be adjudged by the European Court of Justice in Luxembourg. Respecting data privacy, the Charter protects subjects from intrusion and interference by public bodies in case they disrespect private life, including disregard for the privacy of personal data The signatories commit to respect the right to private and family life, which public authorities may not interfere with, except in the interest of national security, public safety or the economic well-being of the country, or for the sake of protecting the public health and the rights and freedoms of others (European Union Agency for Fundamental Rights website).

Under Clause 5(4) of the "Great Repeal Bill" (European Union (Withdrawal) Act 2018), the CFR will not be retained in UK law after exit from the EU (HM Government, November 2018).

2.3 A robust privacy framework for the UK because rooted in international law

This Section discusses Convention 108 on transborder data flows and overviews documents that concern EU-UK data transfers, plus anticipated arrangements for a future data-transfer relationship. Although the plan is for a special EU-UK data agreement, these documents still lack sufficient detail.

2.3.1 Convention 108+ on transborder data flows

One of the more robust solutions to the potential conflicts between the UK and the EU in case of a No-deal Brexit which comes anywhere near being comprehensive is the data protection framework set forth in the Council of Europe's Convention for the Protection of Individuals with regard to Automatic Processing of Personal Data (ETS No. 108), which the UK has already ratified.

The EU's General Data Protection Regulation, Article 45 spells out the basic criteria which the European Commission must follow when assessing the data protection of third countries outside the EU's data protection and privacy regime, when data is transferred from the EU to such country. Section (2)(c) states one such criterion to be "the international commitments the third country [a post-No Deal UK] or international organisation concerned has entered into, or other obligations arising from legally binding conventions or instruments as well as from its participation in multilateral or regional systems, in particular in relation to the protection of personal data".

The UK has already ratified just such a "multilateral or regional system in relation to the protection of personal data" in the Council of Europe's Convention for the Protection of Individuals with regard to Automatic Processing of Personal Data 1981, ETS No. 108 (as modernised by CETS No. 223 [*a.k.a.* "Convention 108+"]). The UK ratified 108+ on 10 October 2018 (Baker, 2018). Convention 108+ touches upon all of the principles of data protection and privacy enshrined in the EU's GDPR. This modernised Convention allows the rechristened "Convention Committee" in CETS No. 223, Chapter VI "to evaluate the effectiveness of the measures it has taken in its law" (modifying ETS No. 108, Article 4); defines new special categories of personal data that require appropriate legal safeguards in order to be processed (modifying ETS No. 108, Article 6); requires the notification of "data breaches which may seriously interfere with the rights and fundamental freedoms of data subjects" without delay to the competent Supervisory Authority (modifying ETS No. 108, Article 7); and strengthens the individual rights of data subjects (modifying ETS No. 108, Article 8 with new Article 9 – "Rights of the data subject").

This means that the European Commission can avail itself of the Convention

Committee as an independent basis for assessing the quality and adequacy of UK data protection law. Greenleaf states that it is not expected that the revised Convention 108 would provide the same level of protection as the GDPR; however it requires the "Convention parties to at least provide protection which the EU would consider 'adequate' under the GDPR" (Greenleaf, 2016:3). This is why the EU endorses Convention 108, and why the UK should continue adhering to this Convention.

Both European Commission officials (anonymised) and MPs in Westminster agree that the UK's ratification of and participation in Convention 108+ is a firm basis on which to expect that the UK can continue to enjoy the EU's approval of adequacy of data protection even after a No-deal Brexit, in that the UK will be bound by an international treaty and multilateral regime of data protection which supersedes its own laws to the contrary. As work on an adequacy decision and/or data protection agreement has not even started yet, and the timelines could exceed two years or more, Convention 108+ might conceivably serve as an interim substitute for a timely adequacy decision by the European Commission.

Jennifer Baker of the International Association of Privacy Professionals, after noting that the former Convention (ETS No. 108) on data privacy rights "has been given an overhaul to bring it into line with the [EU] General Data Protection Regulation", reports that "'[t]he modernized convention will ... provide a unique forum for co-operation in this field at global level,' [according to] Council of Europe Secretary-General Thorbjørn Jagland". According to Baker, the Commission has stated, "It will reflect the same principles as those enshrined in the new EU data protection rules and thus contribute to the convergence towards a set of high data protection standards." She notes that the "Commission sees [Convention 108+] as a way of encouraging 'third countries' to adopt the basic tenets of the GDPR. This could be particularly interesting for the U.K., which will become a third country after [especially a No-deal] Brexit" (Baker, 2018).

What is more, at least one Commission official has admitted that the EU's own data protection regime is based on Convention 108: "it is a living document and it provides for a standard setting process on a very wide range of issues. Even the EU's data protection directive for law enforcement is inspired partly by Convention 108", according to Bruno Gencarelli, head of the data protection unit. Finally, a Commission official speaking off the record conceded that it is "the only international binding instrument ... [that] has elements of convergence and brings third countries much closer to the EU and therefore adequacy [and] it covers all sectors including the security services. If post-Brexit we are to look at making an adequacy assessment of the U.K., the question of national intelligence will be a particularly important and sensitive issue". As a plus, Convention 108+ extends the catalogue of "sensitive" personal data to genetic and biometric data, and individual data rights have been beefed up with a right to withhold consent, a right to be informed without delay of breaches of personal data privacy, and a right to be exempt from decisions affecting oneself based on machine processing only (Baker, 2018).

The UK Parliament has likewise expressed itself on the likelihood of Convention 108+ enabling the UK to meet the Commission's adequacy standards into the future regardless of the terms of Brexit: "[31.8] It is clear from Article 45(c) of the General Data Protection Regulation that the UK acceding to the amended Convention would assist it in obtaining a data adequacy decision after either its exit from the EU or at the end of the planned transition/implementation period, whichever applies" (House of Commons, 12 December 2018). While the UK is confident that the requirements for an adequacy decision are met, the intention is to speed up the process.

2.3.2   Technical note on any EU-UK Data Protection Agreement

It is understood that the UK wishes to maintain the existing arrangements so as to cement a "special relationship" with the EU once it has become a "third country" (HM Government, 7 June 2018). The technical note on the "Benefits of a new data protection agreement", which was presented by the UK government in June 2018, is the UK's first and most comprehensive vision in regards to post-Brexit data transfer. It calls for an agreement which would supersede a mere adequacy decision by creating a special relationship that would empower the UK to participate on EDPB as if the UK were a Member State. Neither party would have any right to prevent the other from enacting further legislation that superseded this agreement (Article 3). This means both parties would be duty bound to deal constructively with challenges. A treaty would provide more continuity than a discretionary executive decision by the Commission (Article 5). A treaty would also give EU citizens more rights in UK courts (Article 7 and 8). Such a treaty would be the only way back onto the European Data Protection Board and the EU's "one-stop shop" mechanism to reduce costs and red tape for businesses by letting them deal with a single "lead supervisory" data protection authority no matter how many Member States a data-processing company might be doing business in (Article 9). Above all this such a treaty would give more protection to companies which would be no longer subject to expensive multiple proceedings or liable to double fines (Article 12 and 13). Finally, the treaty would allow the EU to continue benefitting from the world-beating expertise of the UK's Information Commissioner's Office (ICO) (Article 14), and maintain the UK's influence in EU governing institutions.

This is probably wishful thinking by the UK. Such an agreement would amount to a treaty between two sovereign powers, with the UK co-equal with the EU in international law. The EU is an exclusive club which provides privileges not available to non-Members; it has never offered any such agreement to any third country before. It is speculative if it would amount to more than a mutual adequacy decision like EU-Japan. Also, the EU has shown it wants to discipline the UK for the sin of exiting the EU. The odds favour the EU sticking to its ordinary mechanism.

2.3.3   The Withdrawal Agreement *vs.* a No-deal Brexit

The Withdrawal Agreement of the UK and Northern Ireland from the EU specifically mentions data and information obtained by authorities or official bodies of or in the UK, and processed and transferred between the UK and EU before the end of the Transition Period (Title VII, page 126). The Agreement includes a transition period, which if ratified would provide an extension for organisations to continue processing personal data under existing rules until the end of December 2020. If and only if the Withdrawal Agreement is ratified by the UK parliament does its contents come within the scope of this Blue Paper, otherwise it does not.

The UK Withdrawal Agreement guarantees an "adequacy decision" for the UK until the end of the transition period (31 December 2020). Article 73 states that during this period, from the day the UK leaves the EU (initially the 29 March 2019) until 31 December 2020, the UK will maintain a data protection status quo with the EU. The European Commission is planning to use this time to conduct an assessment of the UK's data protection regime with the aim of providing the UK with a decision on the adequacy of its data protection safeguards. UK negotiators will push for a decision to be finalised near the end of the transition period. Boris Johnson's succession as Prime Minister in July 2019 has increased the likelihood of a No-deal Brexit, due to his uncompromising position on renegotiating the Withdrawal Agreement, and thus that it will leave without a data protection agreement of any type.

In the event that the Withdrawal Agreement is not ratified, the flow of personal data from the EU to the UK could be restricted when Brexit happens. Businesses who wish to transfer personal data from the EU into the UK would need to employ "appropriate safeguards" which were used when personal data is exported outside of the EEA. Examples of such appropriate safeguards include EU Model Clauses and Binding Corporate Rules as discussed in chapter four (HM Government (25 November 2018) [Withdrawal Agreement]).

2.3.4   The Political Declaration

The "Political Declaration Setting Out the Framework for the Future Relationship between the European Union and the United Kingdom" (HM Government and European Council, 25 Nov 2018 [Political Declaration]) recognises the importance of data flows between the two jurisdictions, and of the rules provided by the European Commission on adequacy as to data transfers to third countries. The Political Declaration is nothing more than the declaration over data transfer *inter alia* and contains no legal-binding rules. The document proposes to the EU and UK to commit to a mutual high level of data protection and to a decision of the UK's adequacy by the European Commission by the end of 2020 (Section B 8-10 "Data Protection") (HM Government, 25 November 2018). It states that the Commission will not start up the UK's adequacy assessment until after the UK withdraws, but provides no further details (Paragraph 8-10).

The Commission, while insisting it follows standard procedures, is constructing a bargaining chip in future negotiations with the UK, with the probable intent of threatening interminable delay in reaching an adequacy decision so as to pressurise the UK to concede on other matters of disagreement. One scenario is that, in the event the UK chooses a No-deal Brexit, the Commission could threaten to punish it unless it sticks with certain special arrangements for the Irish border in the Withdrawal Agreement (the so-called "backstop"). Another scenario is that the Commission will demand concessions that would devalue the UK's "bargaining chip" of cooperation on security and intelligence, as part of the wider negotiations (see Chapter Five).

Paragraph 9 of the Political Declaration states that the UK will be establishing its own regulatory regime to enable the international transfer of personal data to the EU in the timeframe of 31 December 2020. Interestingly, it also states, "The future relationship will not affect the Parties' autonomy over their respective personal data protection rules" (Paragraph 9), which indicates that the UK does not intend to set up a regime controlled by the EU, but an independent regulatory framework which aims for "appropriate cooperation between regulators" (Paragraph 10). Achieving independence, while collaborating on certain aspects that would bring the UK benefits, will likely require lengthy negotiations. Unfortunately, the UK needs a fast decision to avoid a "data limbo" once it has become a third country.

2.3.5 Guidance and Notices by HM Government and Parliamentary committees

More than three years after the Brexit referendum, HM Government, Committees of the House of Commons (*viz.*, the Exiting the European Union Select Committee and the Home Affairs Committee), and in the House of Lords (*viz.*, the European Union Committee and the DCMS Committee) have produced Guidances and Notices addressing important aspects of safeguarding personal data and data flows. For example, the UK government lays out in a series of Technical Notices what preparations that citizens, businesses, and the public sector should make to enable the continued flow of personal data between the UK and the EU in the worst-case, No-deal scenario.

HM Government have provided a partial solution already: "In recognition of the unprecedented degree of alignment between the UK and EU's data protection regimes, the UK [government] would at the point of exit continue to allow the free flow of personal data from the UK to the EU. The UK would keep this under review" (HM Government, DCMS, September 2018). This Blue Paper addresses data transfers not covered by this allowance, namely, personal data transferred from the EU to the UK. The European Commission has indicated that no decision on the adequacy of data protection by the UK can be taken until after the UK has exited and is a third country, not a member of the EU. It follows that in the event of a No-deal Brexit, data controllers and processors must find alternative legal bases for transfers of data from the EU to the UK. These bases define the scope of this Paper.

Chapter 3

ADEQUACY OF PERSONAL DATA PROTECTION IN NON-EU COUNTRIES

This chapter reviews the legal basis and criteria for obtaining an "adequacy decision", which is a formal determination by the European Commission that a non-EU country can assure an adequate level of personal data protection in accordance with European law. The effect of a positive decision is that personal data may flow freely from Member States of the European Economic Area (EEA), which includes the EU, to non-EEA countries without any further or alternative safeguards.

An adequacy decision would be the preferred option for the UK, as this mechanism would put all UK organisations that control data ("data controllers") and/or process it ("data processors") in a position to transfer personal data with no or no significant contractual agreements between the several legal entities involved. An analysis of the weaknesses of these arrangements may be used to explain some of the challenges that the UK may face when applying for either an adequacy decision or a more comprehensive scheme.

For this reason we proceed by analysing current adequacy decisions, in particular those involving the United States and Canada (partial adequacy), plus Japan, the first country to obtain an adequacy decision under the new GDPR. From this review, conclusions will be drawn that may address the challenges the UK may face in obtaining adequacy status after Brexit. According to the European Union (Withdrawal) Act 2018, Art. 3(1) & (2), any EU Regulation or Decision or EU tertiary legislation, so far as operative immediately before exit day, shall "form part of domestic law on and after exit day". By the Act's terms, this includes the European Commission's adequacy decisions to the date of Brexit; thus, the only controversy will be over adequacy decisions made by the Commission after Brexit – even in the eventuality of No-deal. Also covered are the implications in case of a non-adequacy decision, and lessons learned.

The European Commission's adequacy decisions on data protection also cover "international [business] organisations", and are not automatic or guaranteed for Big Name global firms such as Dell, BT, and RBS; consequently, they are exploring their options in earnest in the very realistic case that adequacy is denied them (Ram, Megaw and Khan, 2018a). On the one hand, Vera Jourova, EU Commissioner for Justice, Consumers and Gender Equality, which is in charge of data protection, has stated, "We definitely will want, for the sake of business interests, the quickest and most efficient legal framework for the exchange of data with the UK"; on the other hand, Giovanni Buttarelli, Europe's data protection supervisor (EDPS), has warned, "Brexit means a data protection Brexit." Negotiations, he said, could drag on for years (Kostaki, 2019), and he pointed out that the UK will have to queue behind other third countries currently being assessed, such as Mexico, South Korea and India (Khan, 2019). Based on past experience, an adequacy assessment is a complex process and a decision generally takes about two years (techUK et al, 2017).

As at 2013 Kuner counted more than 70 countries that had adopted data protection laws regulating transborder data flows, including all of the EEA countries (Kuner, 2013:10). He also compiled a comprehensive list of binding and non-binding international instruments – laws, regulations, treaties, and private sector agreements – and their provisions in regards to data transfer (Kuner, 2011). As an alternative solution for more effective protection for transborder data flows if an adequacy decision fails, Kuner proposed an "accountability approach" which would "provide incentives for data controllers not to circumvent EU rules" (Kuner, 2009b:10). Ismail also advocates the concept of accountability, which in business organisations should involve the board level, the executive committee, and senior management, supported by employees, business partners, legal counsel and auditors (Ismail, 2013:125-128). The GDPR's increased fines strengthening enforcement is implementing this approach, and in most organisations a governance structure with clear accountability has been established. In practical terms this means unauthorised and non-compliant data transfers will be sanctioned internally, and systematic failure should be detectable through the three lines of defence (*i.e.* the function that owns the risk, risk management and compliance, and independent assurance as the last line of defence).

Bygrave points out that a lack of clarity pertains to the aims of data privacy law (Bygrave, 2014). Although he describes what he calls "the USA and the transatlantic data privacy divide" (pp. 107-116), he claims that the aims are similar on both sides of the Atlantic. Again, this is an important observation, if true, as the UK aims to forge trade deals with the US, and it is essential that an agreement on data transfer can be reached after Brexit.

3.1   Transfers on the basis of adequacy decisions

The European Commission is tasked under GDPR to conduct adequacy assessments "of personal data to a third country or an international organisation". It can "decide that the third country, a territory or one or more specified sectors within that third country, or the international organisation in question ensures [or does not ensure] an adequate level of protection" (Article 45(2)). Article 45(2) and Recital 104 of the GDPR set out a list of criteria for an adequate level of protection of personal data transferred to or through third countries or international organisations, which, if met, exempted them from the need for specific authorisations. The adequacy criteria include these considerations:

(a)   the rule of law, human rights and fundamental freedoms, reckoning-in the effect of the law of public security and public order, defence and national security, and crime;

(b)   effective independent data protection supervision to enforce the law and to provide a mechanism for cooperating with EU Member States' data protection authorities; and adequate means for data subjects to enforce their rights, if necessary through judicial redress; and

(c)   legally binding agreements and/or participation in "multilateral or regional systems" to protect personal data.

A prime consideration in the Commission's adequacy assessment is whether or not the third country has acceded to the Council of Europe's (CoE's) Convention for the Protection of Individuals with regard to Automatic Processing of Personal Data of 28 January 1981 (*a.k.a.* "Data Protection Convention" ETS No. 108),[3] to which all 47 member states of the CoE are parties, as well as non-member states which have received "white list" (adequate) status such as Argentina, Morocco and Uruguay. The importance of the CoE's conventions and protocols to the GDPR scheme is such that the European Council Decision of 9 April 2019 (2019/682) authorised the EU Member States to ratify the latest modernisation of ETS No. 108, namely, the Protocol amending the Convention for the Protection of Individuals with regard to Automatic Processing of Personal Data of 10 October 2018 (CETS No. 223), now largely accomplished.[4] In addition to most EU countries, CETS No. 223 has also been ratified by Andorra, Iceland, Monaco, Norway, the Russian Federation and San Marino, giving these signatories an inside track to a positive adequacy decision by the Commission (Council of Europe website "Chart of signatures and ratifications of Treaty 223").

If these criteria are met by a third country, a territory or a specific sector within this

---

[3]   ETS means European Treaty Series (and CETS means Council of Europe Treaty Series), the "Complete list of the Council of Europe's treaties"; see: https://www.coe.int/en/web/conventions/full-list.

[4]   Ratifiers include 23 of the 28 current EU Member States: Austria, Belgium, Bulgaria, Croatia, Cyprus, Czech Republic, Estonia, Finland, France, Germany, Hungary, Ireland, Italy, Latvia, Lithuania, Luxembourg, Netherlands, Poland, Portugal, Slovenia, Spain, Sweden, and the UK. (Non-ratifiers are Slovakia, Malta, Romania, Denmark, and Greece.)

third country, or an international organisation so as to ensure an adequate level of protection, an adequacy decision can be granted (Article 45(3) and Recital 104 GDPR). Adequacy decisions are not permanent, it should be noted. The Commission is expected to monitor developments in third countries *etc.* on an ongoing basis (Article 43(4)), and conduct periodic reviews of its decisions, once every four years at least. This review should reckon-in findings by the European Parliament, the European Council, and other bodies, and report to the "Article 93 Committee" – a comitology body set up by the EP and Council to collaborate with the Commission to implement the GDPR (Article 45(3) and Recital 106). The full assessment procedure is explained in Article 93(2). (This Article refers to Regulation (EU) No 182/2011 "laying down the rules and general principles concerning mechanisms for control by Member States of the Commission's exercise of implementing powers".) If an adequate level of protection cannot be ensured any longer, the adequacy decision should be repealed, amended or suspended (Article 45(5)), and remediation steps agreed (Article 45(6)). This could happen if the UK repeals the GDPR, for example, or is breaching the criteria on which the decision was awarded.

As at May 2019 the European Commission has recognised thirteen third countries as providing adequate personal data protections under Article 45 of the GDPR (the so-called "white list"): Andorra, Argentina, Canada (commercial organisations), Faroe Islands, Guernsey, Israel, Isle of Man, Japan, Jersey, New Zealand, Switzerland, Uruguay, and the USA (limited to the Privacy Shield). Talks are currently underway with South Korea (European Commission – Adequacy decisions). The Commission's assessment cases and the arguments for and against adequacy in each case are made public. The following Section reviews the adequacy decisions awarded so far in alphabetical order, and analyses the reasons for the decisions, before inquiring whether or not the UK is likely able to meet this standard of assessment.

In the past the process of assessment and the criteria on which adequacy decisions were awarded was not transparent. While some knowledge of the criteria was available, assessments were not treated like EU tender evaluations, where clear criteria and weighting for each criteria is provided as part of the process. Adequacy decisions where often political, based on judgement and the need to support economic relationships and trade, often neglecting enforcement and redress in the case of failure to safeguard personal data. Kuner likewise concluded in 2009 that "the present EU legal framework for 'adequacy' decisions for the international transfer of personal data is inadequate" (Kuner, 2009), and needs reform. His criticisms demanded procedural and substantive changes, as adequacy is: –

- a costly and length process, caused by under-resourcing at the relevant units of the Commission;
- influenced by political factors which make the outcomes unpredictable (*e.g.*, EU-US

adequacy);

- rarely granted – only a relatively small number of countries have received a positive adequacy decision; primarily it is small counties that are on the "white list";
- fraught with a lack of tools and "best practices", absence of standardised checklists, clear procedures and standardised deadlines for the various steps; and
- in need of partial or sectoral adequacy decisions, which would reduce the complexity and increase the speed.

The same issues persist nowadays, and despite improved technology and communications on the Commission's website, little has been done to improve the transparency of the process and the final evaluation criteria used for adequacy decisions. This is why the analysis below of existing adequacy decisions is so important.

Andorra, the first country on the white list, has enshrined a right of privacy in Article 14 of its Constitution. Moreover, Andorra has ratified the Protocol amending the Convention for the Protection of Individuals with regard to Automatic Processing of Personal Data of 10 October 2018 (CETS No. 223). Its legal rules for data protection in the Qualified Law 15/2003 are based on EU Directive 95/46/EC. The Andorran Data Protection Agency, which is independent of the government, has investigatory powers, and judicial remedies are guaranteed (European Commission [Andorra adequacy], 19 October 2010).

Argentina has implemented general and sector-specific rules, as laid down in its Constitution and its Data Protection Act (European Commission [Argentina adequacy], 30 June 2003). This shows that adequacy does not require an alignment to EU data protection law, but only a determination that the relevant protections are implemented and enforcement instruments made available to data transfer subjects. The Commission Decision stressed that an important consideration in its assessment of adequacy was that Argentina's constitution makes privacy a fundamental right.

The **Faroe Islands**, which are a self-governing community under the Kingdom of Denmark, divides all policy domains into two groups – Special Faeroese Affairs and Joint Concerns, which latter are the responsibility of Denmark. This legal and institutional set-up meets the criteria for adequacy because Denmark, as an EU Member State subject to the GDPR Directive, automatically meets the criteria (European Commission [Faroe Islands adequacy], 5 March 2010).

Guernsey, **Jersey**, and the **Isle of Man**, three self-governing islands in the English Channel and the Irish Sea, respectively, often associated with the United Kingdom, are in fact outside its jurisdiction. Though not members of the European Union, they have a special relationship to it, with access to the Customs Union (Guernsey is also part of the Single Market). All three islands ratified the CoE's Data Protection Convention (ETS No. 108), and have enacted a data protection framework based on the standards set out in Directive 95/46/EC. Each island has an independent Data Protection Commissioner (European Commission [Guernsey adequacy], 21 Nov 2003; European Commission [Isle of Man adequacy], 28 April 2004; European Commission [Jersey adequacy], 8 May 2008). These decisions show that the Commission puts some weight on a robust international legal framework.

Israel has no written constitution, like the UK, but a basic law and a large body of case law. In conjunction with the Israeli Privacy Protection Act and decisions by the government, as well as financial and health sector-specific regulation, the Commission has deemed Israel EU-adequate (European Commission [Israel adequacy], 31 January 2011).

New Zealand like the UK has no written constitution. The Bill of Rights Act 1990, the Human Rights Act 1993, and the Privacy Act 1993 are particularly cited in the Commission's decision, indicating the value the Commission gives to human rights in the context of data protection (European Commission [New Zealand adequacy], 19 December 2012).

Switzerland has legal data protection standards both at Federal and cantonal level, and also has a Federal Commissioner with powers to investigate and intervene (European Commission [Switzerland adequacy], 26 July 2000). It is clear from this decision that the Commission wants to see not just a law on the books, but a forceful regulator fully equipped with the authority to enforce it.

Uruguay sets out in Article 72 of its Constitution "the right to the protection of personal data is inherent to the human being", plus its legal standards are based on Directive 95/46/EC. Special acts to regulate databases and public registries contain data protection provisions. Uruguay's membership of the American Convention of Human Rights (since 22 November 1969), which lays down a right of privacy (Article 30), and its adoption of the Council of Europe's Convention for the Protection of Individuals with regard to Automatic Processing of Personal Data (ETS No. 108) reinforces its commitment to meet the requirements of Directive 95/46/EC (European Commission [Uruguay adequacy], 21 August 2012).

3.2   Partial or sector-specific adequacy decisions

The Commission has adopted a tough stance on privacy in international trade. Respecting privacy is a condition for stable, secure and competitive global commercial flows. Privacy is not a commodity to be traded (European Commission, 14 October 2015:7.). This Section will analyse how the UK can shape its data protection alternatives with third countries that may lack full EU-adequacy under GDPR. The USA and Canada have been deemed to provide only partially adequate protection, which is analysed in the following Section.

3.2.1   United States: Reasons for the failure of Safe Harbour and some weaknesses of the Privacy Shield

The "Safe Harbour" decision, which was agreed between the EU and US in 2000, was challenged in 2013 by privacy campaigner Max Schrems. As a result, it was declared invalid by the European Court of Justice in 2015 in the *Max Schrems v. Data Protection Commissioner case* (The Court (Grand Chamber) Judgement, 6 October 2015). The CJEU ruled that the Safe Harbour framework did not provide an adequate level of protection "essentially equivalent" to that provided in the EU, and in 2015 the Court invalidated the Commission's adequacy decision.

The complaint was launched with the Irish DPA after Facebook's European HQ in Ireland transferred data to the US. Schrems argued that the US government did not sufficiently protect European citizen's data from state surveillance (such as the PRISM surveillance programme). The CJEU had ruled in 2000 that the Safe Harbour scheme was sufficient; however, the High Court of Ireland sought guidance from the European Commission whether it might overrule the CJEU's decision following the Snowden revelations in 2015.[5] The CJEU found that public interest and law enforcement regulations in the US can override the Safe Harbour if a conflict is found between the two, whence it arrived at its new ruling, which made data transfers under Safe Harbour unlawful. As a consequence, companies such as Google, Microsoft, Apple and Facebook were no longer able to rely on self-certification, but had to take refuge in standard contractual clauses to authorise data transfers outside of Europe.

The Privacy Shield became operational on 1 August 2016 and included the following changes (European Commission, 12 July 2016):

(1)   stronger obligations on companies receiving personal data from EU data subjects (*e.g.,*

---

[5]   In 2013 Edward Snowden revealed that the UK's Government Communications Headquarters (GCHQ) was secretly intercepting, processing and storing the data of millions of people's private communications, although these people were clearly of no intelligence interest (the "Tempora" programme). The USA's National Security Agency (NSA) and other countries' intelligence agencies shared these data. These practices took place without public awareness or consent, and without any legal basis or proper safeguards (Harding, 2016).

(2)   safeguards and transparency obligations on the US government when accessing data (to rule out indiscriminate mass surveillance on personal data transferred);

(3)   (3) a redress mechanism for citizens whose data have been misused (including an Ombudsman mechanism and Alternative Dispute resolution); and

(4)   an annual joint review mechanism between the European Commission and the US Department of Commerce to monitor the agreement.

An alternative post-Brexit solution to protecting privacy in the exchange of personal data between the EU and the UK might resemble the EU-US Privacy Shield, which requires US businesses that voluntarily choose to participate to abide by European data protection principles. Although such a self-certification approach might work for the UK, a general adequacy decision is preferable for both the UK government and UK organisations, as it is less time-consuming, costly and uncertain (European Parliament, 2018:30). It is well-known that the Privacy Shield does little or nothing to protect the privacy of EU citizens' personal data (Kuner, 2017). Nevertheless, the EU is effectively held hostage by the power and importance of the US in and to the world economy; meaning that data exchanges between the EU and the US cannot be prohibited, come what may. "At the global level, the EU's involvement in multilateral bargaining is shaped by its relationship to the US. The two great trade powers have been engaged for years in what the rest of the world sees as a battle of titans, whereby each side tries to ensure a continued balance in market access to the other side through trade and regulatory deals" (Meunier and Nicolaïdis, 2006:911). The UK is an important market, too, but has far less bargaining power than the US, and is more dependent on the EU (Brinded, 2017:3).

Even if the Privacy Shield was set up in case the UK cannot achieve full adequacy, there are concerns about the legality of this framework, especially whether it will meet the new and higher standards of the GDPR, even after the improvements it made to the Safe Harbour framework (European Commission – EU-US data transfers; see also Art. 29 WP, 13 April 2016; EDPS, 30 May 2016). A 5 July 2018 European Parliament Resolution recommended, after hearing views from the Committee on Civil Liberties, Justice and Home Affairs, and various other sources (including court cases), that the Commission suspends the EU-US Privacy Shield if certain corrective measures are not taken by the Department of Commerce (European Parliament, 5 July 2018). In addition, the Article 29 Working Party gave an Opinion (Art. 29 WP (13 April 2016) "Opinion 01/2016 on the EU-U.S. Privacy Shield draft adequacy decision", WP 238.) which made recommendations for both the commercial and national-security aspects of the Privacy Shield (Art. 29 WP, 28 Nov 2017).

The Privacy Shield has been outlined in the most comprehensive Decision of the Commission so far (112 pages) which made 13 recommendations published in

Communication (2013/847) (European Commission – USA (limited to the Privacy Shield) adequacy], 12 July 2016, Recital 12). The European Commission reviews the arrangement on an annual basis. Although the second annual review purported to find that the Privacy Shield ensures an adequate level of protection for personal data, the Commission made ten urgent recommendations for improvement including: to proactively monitor compliance by certified companies; to focus on the detection of false claims by new applicants; to develop additional guidance; to improve the complaints-handling and resolution process; to install an Ombudsman; and that the US adopts a comprehensive system of privacy and data protection and becomes a Party to Convention 108+ (European Commission, 19 December 2018). The Privacy Shield has recently come under attack, as exemplified by the investigations into the Facebook / Cambridge Analytica case. The UK ought to draw some lessons from the key concerns raised and implement additional mitigating safeguards to address lessons learnt from the failure of the previous Safe Harbour agreement. These could help the UK obtain an adequacy decision, lest the similar concerns discussed in this Blue Paper lead to a negative decision by the Commission.

So, what are the lessons learned from the "special" EU-US adequacy decision? The landmark judgment of the CJEU in *Schrems v. Data Protection Commissioner* (CJEU, 6 October 2015) that invalidated Safe Harbour affirmed the importance of international data transfers in EU law and defined an adequate level of data protection. An interesting takeaway for the UK is that the EU-US negotiations to replace Safe Harbour took place in secrecy, and the political pressure to enact the replacement (Privacy Shield) as quickly as possible was high (Sheftalovich, 2016). This case also illustrates how many legal disputes concerning data transfers are concealed political power plays (Kuner, 2017). The CJEU's formal decision was that Privacy Shield provides a level of data protection that is "essentially equivalent" to that of EU law (Commission Implementing Decision (12 July 2016) 2016/1250). Also, an international agreement concerning data exchanges between law enforcement authorities (the so-called "Umbrella Agreement"), and changes to US law – the Judicial Redress Act of 2015 (Public Law No. 114-126 (02/24/2016)) – that grant further rights to EU individuals had to be implemented.

Kuner argues that data transfer regulation needs to go beyond "formalistic measures and legal fictions", and calls illusory the view that there is an effective protection of EU personal data transferred around (Kuner, 2017:884-885). He concluded that the data protection concepts in the EU's adequacy decisions regarding the US have influenced US practice (Kuner, 2017:894). The Privacy Shield is similar to Safe Harbour. It is based on a set of principles derived from EU law, which US Companies voluntarily self-certify their adherence to with the US Department of Commerce. Compliance is policed by the Federal Trade Commission (FTC – Privacy Shield, and is to be monitored by the European Commission (European Commission – EU-US data transfers). US companies doing business in the EU have increased their awareness of the GDPR's new rules, which are far more stringent, with significant fines and penalties, and provide redress mechanisms for users, customers, and representative bodies to pursue litigation (Lambert, 2018).

The ICO has clarified that existing EU adequacy decisions, including the Privacy Shield, will continue to be lawful mechanisms to export data outside the UK (HM Government, 23 April 2019). Participants from the US with establishments in the UK can rely on the Privacy Shield no longer than 31 October 2019, which would mean that the UK should have alternative mechanisms in place by then in case of a No-deal Brexit (Privacy Shield Framework, 2019).

The EU has taken an international leadership role respecting privacy and human rights, and many countries and multinational businesses have been mirroring and implementing EU principles (Weber and Staiger, 2017:22). The wide territorial scope of the GDPR requires US businesses to apply EU rules across their organisational group, because they offer services to EU customers and collect their data (Weber and Staiger, 2017:3). The UK's continued alignment to the EU framework should ease adequacy arrangements with "third countries" which have adopted EU principles.

3.2.2   Canada: Partial adequacy decision

In Canada, only private organisations falling under the scope of the Canadian Personal Information Protection and Electronic Documents Act 2000 ("the Canadian Act") and use personal data for commercial activities have access to personal data from the EU under the Commission's decision. The adequacy decision also supports the Comprehensive Economic Trade Agreement (CETA) that was recently negotiated between the EU and Canada.

It its decision the Commission deemed the Canadian Act adequate (European Commission [Canada (commercial organisations) adequacy], 20 December 2001), even though it applies to the private sector only, to organisations that disclose personal data outside Canada, while exempting the public sector, employment data, and data used for non-commercial purposes. The Commission stressed that Canada also formally adheres to the "OECD Guidelines on the Protection of Privacy and Transborder Flows of Personal Data" (29 June 1984, revised in 2013) and the "UN Guidelines Concerning Computerized Personal Data Files" (14 December 1990).

As the agreement with Canada is for commercial organisations only, they UK must decide if this is sufficient. As a starting position, however, the UK is expecting a full adequacy decision.

3.2.3   Future inadequate third-country trading partners of the UK

Data flows are not confined to UK-EU traffic, but necessarily involve third countries "offshore" (*i.e.* internationally) and outside the EU. As the UK negotiates its own trade agreements with these countries, it must extend its agreements with the EU on data transfer to them. In default of the adequacy of such extension to any third country, the GDPR provides some alternative data protection mechanisms – contractual clauses, Codes of conduct, certifications – which can be more efficiently instituted through the EDPB – if the UK has a seat (Vanberg and Maunick, 2018; Lawson, 2018; House of Lords, HM Government, 18 July 2017). The UK advertising lobby, notably the Direct Marketing Association and the Advertising Association, and even global technology firms such as Google, Facebook and Twitter have argued that Britain having a voice in Europe on data would benefit its industries and consumers (Frean, 2018:43). It remains to be seen, but is unlikely that the UK will be granted voting rights on the EDPB, and may not even merely be given observer status, like Norway and Iceland.

On the other side of the adequacy spectrum, the UK should strive for mutual adequacy agreements, as between the UK and India or Australia, deploying the GDPR panoply similarly to the mutual EU-Japan adequacy agreement, as safer and more comprehensive. However, this could be very time-consuming and may prove impracticable; therefore, alternative mechanisms may need to be deployed.

The UK will not have or be able to maintain a mutual adequacy relationship with the EU if data protection is not provided-for in third countries, in advance of trade negotiations with the UK, within a GDPR-adequate framework. What role will the EDPB have in implementing such a framework? In many cases the third country will never achieve EU-level data protection adequacy; thus, data flows between the UK and such a third country will not be allowable (if the UK would maintain its own adequacy relationship with the EU), unless handled by private parties under the GDPR's alternative mechanisms. The EDPB will become useful, not for what it might recommend to the Commission under GDPR Art. 70(s) about a third country's adequacy, which *ex hypothesi* is inadequate, but for what guidance the EDPB might give to private parties under Art. 70(e)—(j) concerning how they can meet their duties under Arts. 28, 40-41, 42-43 or 49.

Reviewing global legal frameworks for data protection, Kuner concluded that EU data protection law "has both economic motivations (promoting the free flow of data) and human rights motivations (protecting fundamental rights to data protection)" (Kuner, 2013:20). He identified a wide range of data protection instruments that regional organisations outside the EU have adopted, *e.g.* the APEC Privacy Framework (APEC, 2017) or Convention 108 (CoE, 1981); model laws, *e.g.* International Law Commission (ICL, 2019); international guidelines, *e.g.* OECD Privacy Guidelines (OECD, 2013) or UNCTAD Data

Protection regulations and international data flows (UNCAD, 2016); and private sector initiatives, *e.g.* ICC Data Protection Principles of Accountability (ICC, 2012). He also wondered whether organisations such as the WTO, UNESCO, or the International Telecommunications Union should be working toward creating a global data protection standard; these agencies may be too specialised to produce a diverse and multi-faceted data protection standard (Kuner, 2009a). This is a good idea which has been discussed for more than a decade, but the UK has little time and must base its privacy framework on the GDPR, which has raised the bar for data protection around the world and is seen by many as the gold standard for data protection (Buttarelli, 2016:77-78; Heim, 2014:8).

3.3   Japan: First mutual adequacy decision

Japan has become the first foreign state which has counter-vetted the EU for data protection adequacy. The European Commission successfully concluded its negotiation on mutual adequacy of data protection with Japan on 17 July 2018 (European Commission, 17 July 2018). The reciprocal recognition was made in the context of the EU-Japan Economic Partnership Agreement (EPA) that was finalised on 23 January 2019 and entered into force on 1 February 2019, which underlines the importance of free data flows for the export of goods and services (European Commission website "EU-Japan Economic Partnership Agreement").

The EU has not only become "a formidable power in trade", but it is also becoming "a power through trade" and can use this as "a bargaining chip to obtain changes in the domestic policy of its trading partners, from labour standards to human rights, and more general to shape new patterns of global governance." (Meunier and Nicolaidis, 2006:2). As the recent EU adequacy decisions have demonstrated, data protection is an important element intimately tied to trade negotiations and agreements. It remains to be seen if post-Brexit Britain will, like the EU, become an advocate for robust data protection when negotiating future trade deals, or compromise human rights and other social aspects for the sake of commercial gain.

This was not only the first adequacy decision granted on the basis of the GDPR, which came into force on 25 May 2018; but per Věra Jourová, EU Commissioner for Justice, Consumers and Gender Equality, it also created "the world's largest area of safe data flows". It is expected that another adequacy review will take place after two years (European Commission, 23 January 2019). To achieve this adequacy decision, Japan was obliged to add further safeguards before each other's personal data protection regime could be recognised as actually equivalent (European Commission and PPC, 23 January 2019). The additional safeguards included:

(1)   supplementary rules to bridge the differences between the two data protection regimes, which will be enforced by the Personal Information Protection Commission (PPC), Japan's data protection authority, and by the Japanese courts, and covering the protection of sensitive data, the vindication of individual rights, and the enforcement of the safeguarding rules under the aegis of which EU personal data may be transferred from Japan to a third country.

(2)   a complaint-handling mechanism operated by the PPC to investigate and properly dispose of complaints from European data subjects.

(3)   assurances that Japanese public authorities will be restricted from accessing personal data for criminal law enforcement and national security purposes through mechanisms of independent oversight and redress.

(European Commission, 23 Jan 2019 [Japan adequacy])

Japan only recently implemented the Act on the Protection of Personal Information (APPI), which then was amended and came into force on 30 May 2017 (European Commission, 23 January 2019 [Japan adequacy]), yet despite its recency, it still proved inadequate without further modification to protect personal data up to the EU standard. The UK, too, has only recently implemented its own Data Protection Act 2018, which purports to provide adequate safeguards of EU citizens' personal data, especially when transferred to a third country outside the EU, a sore point in Brussels.

The trade agreement context presages the increasing importance of free but safe data flows for close economic relationships and trade, a lesson that post-Brexit Britain would do well to heed. As the UK is seeking a trade agreement with the EU, an EU adequacy decision is bound to be a precondition of final agreement in order to win the confidence allowing contemporary digital-economy trade negotiations to reach a mutually satisfactory conclusion. Graham Greenleaf, analysing the mutual adequacy decisions of the EU and Japan, identified a mix of criteria forming the basis of adequacy assessments. These derive partly from the GDPR, from the CJEU's decision in the *Schrems* case, and from Art. 29 WP Opinions. Interestingly, where the Commission's assessment reaches a negative conclusion, as has happened twice in relation to India, no recommendation is forwarded to the EDPB, which issues no Opinion, and little is known about the reasons for the negative assessment (Greenleaf, 2017).

3.4   Likelihood of a non-adequacy decision for the UK

The Commission will surely demand of a post-Brexit UK adequate safeguards when transferring data to third countries, dispute and redress mechanisms for EU residents, and restrictions on accessing personal data for intelligence purposes. It is noteworthy that the UK Data Protection Act omitted to cite the processor as duty-bound to safeguard data transferred to third parties; therefore, it is a question if controller-processor contracts can at least potentially release processors from the duties of controllers under Article 75 ("Transfers on the basis of appropriate safeguards") of the Data Protection Act 2018, which states, "A transfer of personal data to a third country or an international organisation is based on there being appropriate safeguards where—the controller, having assessed all the circumstances surrounding transfers of that type of personal data to the third country or international organisation, concludes that appropriate safeguards exist to protect the data" (DPA 2018). This differs materially from Article 46 ("Transfers subject to appropriate safeguards") of the GDPR, which states, "In the absence of [an adequacy decision], a controller or processor may transfer personal data to a third country or an international organisation only if the controller *or processor* has provided appropriate safeguards, and on condition that enforceable data subject rights and effective legal remedies for data subjects are available" (GDPR 2016).

Article 46 imposes a legal duty on controllers *and processors* that they shall have "provided appropriate safeguards" before transferring EU citizens' data to third countries, breach of which is remediable presumably against processors as well as controllers. This provision's implementation in DPA Article 75, however, makes only the controller responsible (unless common law rules make up for omission of the processor). Ordinarily, correction of DPA defects could have been effected through direct appeal to the CJEU. It remains to be seen, however, if Brexit's extinction of CJEU jurisdiction will allow "daylight" to open up between the UK Act and EU Regulation, as even small differences in liability may yield big differences in *practical* data protection. The UK has an interest in keeping its adequacy under EU law; nevertheless, UK courts may consider themselves obligated to give UK defendants the benefit of UK law as written (see Lee, 2018).

The foregoing review of the Commission's adequacy decisions directly implicates the UK, and offers some useful lessons to any post-Brexit UK government struggling with the complicated issues of trade with the EU. Although no formal application has been made, as the European Commission has required the UK to become a "third country" before starting an assessment, the current process is non-transparent (and possibly politicised) and requires reform, as discussed by Kuner. India has been rejected twice outright without detailed explanation, while the US and Japan were deemed presumptively adequate, pending implementation of conditions necessary to meet the EU standard. The inference must be that political and economic bargaining power plays an important part in the EU's adequacy determinations, which the UK had better take into account.

The UK lacks the bargaining power of the US and possibly Japan, yet it has implemented much of the EU's data protection law already, which is a head-start in trade negotiations. To date, the UK has implemented General Data Protection Regulation 2016/679 and EU Data Protection Directive 2016/680 (Law Enforcement Directive) in form of the Data Protection Act 2018, which has been in force since 25 May 2018. The UK previously transposed the Privacy and Electronic Communications Directive (2002/58/EC), and its five amendments, in the Privacy and Electronic Communications (EC Directive) Regulations 2003 (PECR). Because the UK follows the common law, and not the codification method of the Continent, its pre-EU legal privacy framework, such as it was, had accumulated "haphazardly" in a body of statutes, conventions and judicial decisions. The European Communities Act 1972 gave European law great impact on UK data protection law; however, Brexit could end this if the UK is not careful how changes to its common law may creep in. Indeed, a study commissioned by the European Parliament concluded that the UK should have to follow the relevant case law of the CJEU as part of UK-EU adequacy negotiations (European Parliament, 2018:24).

Like countries that have been assessed adequate by the EU, the UK has an independent Supervisory Authority for data protection, the Information Commissioner's Office (ICO), which provides guidance, handles tens of thousands of complaints each year, and has power to impose fines and take other enforcement measures. The ICO employs around 200 lawyers, analysts, investigators and others to ensure data protection compliance (McGoogan, 2017). Although the ICO's position of influence and important role might be weakened after Brexit, it still meets all the criteria set out for an independent regulatory authority as at the time of writing.

The review of existing adequacy decisions shows that the data protection law of a third country, which the UK will be after Brexit, must be considered in a wider context when assessing its adequacy. For example, unlike Argentina, whose constitution makes personal privacy a fundamental right, the UK acknowledges such a right only through its accession to Convention 108+ and membership of the ECHR. If the UK should pursue the proposal to leave the ECHR after Brexit, this could cause problems of a scope that may attaint more than just EU-adequacy.

Passions have been running high between different political and cultural factions within the UK, as between the UK and EU. Rational and economic arguments have often lagged behind, and a danger exists that this process could overtake data protection and privacy. The Snowden revelations of the scope and magnitude of mass surveillance programmes run by the US National Security Agency primarily, but also the UK's Government Communications Headquarters (GCHQ) have galvanised a public debate on intelligence gathering and its violation of individual privacy. It is an open question if human rights treaties like the ECHR apply to foreign surveillance (Milanovic, March 2014), but if they do, the ECHR may provide some protection against the collection and use of personal data, in Article 8 on the right of respect for privacy and family life, home and correspondence. The UK should beware abrogation of it, or even non-compliance with the judgments of the European Court of Human Rights, whilst leaving the CJEU at the same time, lest the controversy that has already erupted justifies the European Commission in strategically prolonging the UK's adequacy assessment.

To plan for Brexit and to minimise their exposure to risk in the case of a "not adequate" decision as part of a No-deal Brexit, or in case of endless delays by the EU in reaching a decision, UK companies are drawing up contingency plans for their infrastructure and data. Software-as-a-service and hosting-providers are even considering moving their data to the EU. Ireland and the Netherlands have emerged as frontrunners where to set up data hubs (Ram, Megaw, and Khan, 2018b). According to Frontier Economics, "75% of UK cross-border data flows are with EU partner countries", and securing an adequacy decision is identified as a business necessity (Frontier Economics, 2017:37). Ruth Boardman, joint head of the International Privacy and Data Protection Group at the law firm Bird & Bird, has said, "It would be a big political statement for the UK not to get adequacy" (Newscabal, 2018). Tom Thackray of the CBI employers' group commented that "if no transition deal is agreed, the UK's potential £240bn data economy is at risk of isolation" (Thompson and Parker, 2017).

If no adequacy decision is forthcoming by the end of the Brexit process (or a transition period), then transfers of personal data from the EU to the UK may be restricted and have to be undertaken using one of the appropriate alternative safeguards. Article 46 of the GDPR lists Binding Corporate Rules, the Commission's standard data protection contractual clauses (or model clauses), the Supervisory Authorities' authorised standard data protection clauses or contractual clauses as such safeguards (see also Kuner, 2017). These will be analysed below in Chapter Four. It should be noted, however, that all organisations must review their existing data flows from the EU into the UK and consider preparing themselves to implement all appropriate safeguards.

3.5 Conclusions: Lessons learned

To obtain an adequacy decision from the European Commission takes more than just having a functional legal framework for data protection and an independent Supervisory Authority in place. As discussed above, the process and criteria for adequacy are not very transparent, and political motivations and bargaining could delay the process. As noted above, data protection must also be viewed in the wider context of human rights standards, employment rights, fundamental freedoms, national security, and participation in multilateral regimes such as the Council of Europe. "[T]he European Commission will need to assess the adequate level of protection that is offered by the UK in light of the GDPR's new requirements, which includes assessing the rule of law and the protection of human rights in the field of public security, defence, national security and criminal and the access of public authorities to personal data" (Proust, 2019). The UK, then, still has a problem in that there is no simple checklist that the Commission's assessors use. It remains to be seen whether the UK will be able to mitigate or rectify some of the issues that have arisen in recent cases in the CJEU, lest it complicates obtaining an EU adequacy decision in a commercially useful timeframe.

Prime Minister Theresa May's long-standing opposition to the ECHR (Conservative Home, 2016; Worley, 2016) does not favour a positive EU adequacy decision post-Brexit. Her electoral manifesto concession did not close the door on future withdrawal: "Theresa May has said the UK will remain signatories [sic] to the European Convention of Human Rights *for the next Parliament*", leaving unresolved what happens after that (Osbourne, 2017 [emphasis added]). Her successor, Boris Johnson, is known to be even more Eurosceptic than she. Likewise a potential snag is the UK's data-sharing practices under the "Five Eyes" executive agreement with the USA, Canada, Australia and New Zealand. Doubts over just such matters were shared by numerous witnesses in hearings before the European Union Committee of the House of Lords. So long as the UK was a member of the EU, it was "automatically adequate"; however, some incidents have shown that the UK was "not seen as being a gold standard", and national security activities "could be used as a reason for arguing that the UK ought not to be [assessed as] adequate" (House of Lords, 18 July 2017:27).

PART II

Alternative solutions for data transfer

It is a capital mistake to theorise before one has data.
– Sherlock Holmes, "A Study in Scarlett"

Chapter 4

ALTERNATIVE SOLUTIONS FOR DATA TRANSFER IN CASE OF A NON-ADEQUACY DECISION

In the absence of an adequacy decision or an EU-UK data protection agreement, the GDPR allows other mechanisms for international data transfers by individual organisations acting on their own: the provision of "appropriate safeguards" or derogation. These mechanisms and how they may be applied by organisations in a post-Brexit Britain are analysed in this chapter.

4.1   Appropriate safeguards for international data transfers

Brexit means that the UK will become a "third country" from the standpoint of EU law, its full implementation of the GDPR in form of the Data Protection Act 2018 notwithstanding. The third country, any territory and specified sector within it, or an international organisation, must meet an adequate level of data protection before transfers of personal data to this third country or organisation can take place without ongoing authorisation (Recital 103). An adequacy decision for the UK by the European Commission if not forthcoming (Article 45(3) GDPR), data transfers may still be possible through provision of appropriate safeguards and "on condition that enforceable data subject rights and effective legal remedies for data subjects are available" (Article 46 GDPR). Appropriate safeguards include:[6]

- Legally binding and enforceable (contractual) instruments governing data transfers strictly between public authorities (Article 46(2)(a) GDPR). Note well: these instruments should provide data subjects with enforceable rights or effective legal

---

[6]   These available instruments for data transfer from the EEA to the UK have been also confirmed by EDPB (12 February 2019) "Information note on data transfers under the GDPR in the event of a no-deal Brexit", p. 2-4.

remedies, including administrative and judicial redress and claims for compensation, in the Union or in a third country (GDPR Recital 108)).

- Legally Binding Corporate Rules (BCRs) governing transactions between EU and overseas divisions of a corporate group (*e.g.*, franchises) (Article 46(2)(b), Article 47 GDPR).
- Standard data protection clauses (or Standard Contractual Clauses (SCC)) adopted by the Commission (Article 46(2)(c) GDPR) or Member States' Supervisory Authorities and approved by the Commission (Article 46(2)(d) GDPR).
- Codes of conduct (Article 46(2)(e), Article 40).
- Data protection certification mechanisms, marks and seals (Article 46(2)(f), Article 42) (ICO website "International Transfers").

Without either an adequacy decision or any of the safeguards listed above, data transfers can only take place if some derogation for specific situations as detailed in Article 49 applies.

The following Sections analyse these different mechanisms in case the European Commission should decline to grant the UK an adequacy decision, and no special EU-UK data protection agreement has been agreed. The checklist in the Executive Summary lists the various alternative options.

4.1.1   Standard contractual clauses

In the absence of an adequacy decision by the European Commission, standard contractual data protection clauses may be substituted as an alternative method for ensuring adequacy, to allow a transfer to go forward. Article 28 GDPR [Processor] (and Recital 81 of GDPR) provides that where a data processor carries out any processing on behalf of a data controller, the controller must have a prior specific or general written authorisation between the two parties. If processors engage with sub-processors for processing activities, the same obligations as between the controller and processor must apply (Article 28(4) GDPR). The data controller can enter into an individual contract (referred to as "data processing agreement", "service contract", or "data transfer agreement" for intra-company data transfers) or rely on standard contractual clauses (SCC or "model [contract] clause") which have been either adopted by the European Commission or by a Member State's Supervisory Authority and approved by the Commission. This mechanism offers sufficient safeguards of data protection for the data to be transferred internationally. Article 28(3) lays out what the SCCs must stipulate: at a minimum, the following two clauses must be included:

- the data processer "processes the personal data only on documented instructions from the controller"; and

- the data processor must have "sufficient guarantees to implement appropriate technical and organisational measures" (Article 28(1) GDPR) to prevent unauthorised or unlawful processing of, and accidental loss or damage of personal data.

Article 28 allocates responsibility for publishing SCCs to the European Commission (Article 28(7)) and to the Member States' Supervisory Authority (Article 28(8)), which would be the ICO in case of the UK.

The European Commission has adopted two sets of model clauses[7] for data transfer to "third countries"/ non-EU countries, namely:

- EU Controller to non-EU or EEA controller (Set I) (Commission Decision 2001/497/EC), as amended by EU Controller to non-EU or EEA controller (Set II) (Commission Decision 2004/915/EC;

- EU Controller to non-EU or EEA processor (Set I) (Commission Decision 2010/87/EU).

No SCCs have been adopted yet (although a draft is under consideration) for data transfers from:

- EU Processors to non-EU or EEA processors (*e.g.* a cloud provider such as Amazon, which may want to transfer personal data to Japan for example), and

- EU controllers or EU processors to non-EU or EEA sub-processors (Art. 29WP, WP214, 11 April 2018).

The House of Lords' European Union Committee was informed in hearings that SCCs are "the most commonly used way of transferring data because [they require] less effort … you sign a contract and then you have a mechanism for transferring data" (House of Lords, 18 July 2017:p29). Although the SCC method of compliance is popular for intra-group transfers, as it merely requires adding data protection clauses to a single master contract; however, Nigel Parker at the law-firm Allen & Overy criticised it a "depressing exercise that involves a lot of companies putting in place a lot of paperwork", and that "the contract changes don't improve citizens' data protection, but merely fulfil a regulatory purpose" (Trentmann, 2019).

The UK Government's No-deal Guidance recognises the EU's SCCs in UK law, and gives the ICO power to issue new clauses (HM Government, 23 April 2019). Due to the uncertainty of an adequacy decision, the ICO should urgently begin development of model

---

[7]   See also European Commission website – Standard Contractual Clauses (SCC).   Available at https://ec.europa.eu/info/law/law-topic/data-protection/international-dimension-data-protection/standard-contractual-clauses-scc_en (accessed January 2019).

European Commission website – "Model contracts for the transfer of personal data to third countries". Available at https://ec.europa.eu/info/law/law-topic/data-protection/data-transfers-outside-eu/model-contracts-transfer-personal-data-third-countries_en (accessed January 2019).

clauses for the cases of processor-to-subprocessor and processor-to-cloud-services-providers outside the UK/EU. The big question is what happens if the UK develops its own adequacy standards and shares data with countries which it, but not the EU, has determined to be adequate. If the UK will enter into trade negotiations independently with non-EU countries, then this will be a major issue not only in those negotiations, but in the UK's continuing adequacy for the EU. The European Commission may look askance at data being transferred from the EU to the UK and then onwards to India or China. The UK must therefore ensure that its own international and "onward transfer" regimes provide levels of protection equivalent to the EU's, and match EU processes and criteria in making its own adequacy decisions. This will form a key part of the EU's adequacy assessment of the UK's data protection regime, as after the UK exits to become a third country, automatic alignment with EU law will cease. If it is a start, the UK Government's No-deal Guidance pledges to preserve existing EU adequacy decisions post-Brexit, deal or no (HM Government, 23 April 2019).

The flow of data from non-EU countries into the UK is also regulated by foreign jurisdictions, which have their own rules on the transfer of data internationally. This means that the UK enjoys the following post-Brexit options concerning data transfer:

(a)   to keep on relying on (in effect "transposing") the EU's adequacy decisions, as if they were the ICO's, into the indefinite future; utilising the alternative mechanisms that the GDPR has to offer (just as the EU does) in cases of no-adequacy decisions; or else

(b)   to ignore (*i.e.* quit "transposing") EU adequacy decisions, and rely on the UK's own legal arrangements with non-EU third countries, which may entail utilising the GDPR's alternative mechanisms much more extensively in order to maintain its own adequacy with the EU.

4.1.2   New GDPR mechanisms: approved codes of conduct and accredited third-party certifications

Appropriate safeguards for data transfers may be also furnished by Codes of conduct (Article 40-41 GDPR) by and certification procedures (Article 42-43 GDPR), which should in particular assist specific requirements in various sectors and the needs of micro-companies and SMEs. These methods will only work, however, if they contain binding and enforceable commitments to data subjects by the organisations in third countries. The European Data Protection Board (EDPB) has produced specific guidelines[8] on the proper accreditation of certification bodies (EDPB, 4 June 2019 [Guidelines 4/2018]), on certification criteria

---

8   A comprehensive list of all EDPB documents is available at https://edpb.europa.eu/our-work-tools/our-documents_en (accessed June 2019).

(EDPB, 4 June 2019 [Guidelines 1/2018]), on the adoption of Codes of conduct, covering acceptance criteria for codes and requirements for issuing bodies (EDPB, 4 June 2019 [Guidelines 1/2019]). Codes of conduct, by the bye, are voluntary self-regulations allowing businesses to demonstrate industry-specific accountability to Member State Supervisory Authorities. They can be crafted through industry associations or trade bodies representing controllers, but must be monitored by independent accreditors and approved by the Supervisory Authorities, or provided with general validity by the European Commission (EDPB, 4 June 2019; ICO – Codes of Conducts). Certification is also voluntary and follows a similar accreditation process; however, it governs more specific processing activities and can be issued only to the data controllers or processors involved in them (EDPB, 4 June 2019; ICO – Certifications). Both schemes are expected to become operational in autumn 2019.

Codes of conduct must be submitted to the competent Supervisory Authority, which must provide an opinion on whether it complies with the GDPR, then approve the draft Code (Article 40(5)) GDPR). If the Code relates to processing in multiple Member States, the competent Supervisory Authorities must seek an opinion from the EDPB on whether the draft Code provides adequate safeguards (Article 40(7)). The Commission, upon due examination, may decide to adopt Codes recommended by the EDPB as having general validity within the EU, then make those Codes publicly available (Article 40(8-11)). A Code-issuing body that is accredited by a Supervisory Authority is responsible for monitoring compliance with the Code (Article 41(1)).

It is unclear what role the UK's ICO will play post-Brexit in the acceptance process for National Codes, and in particular Transnational Codes, given that it will have to cooperate with EU national Supervisory Authorities, then submit the approved draft Code to the EDPB, of which it is no longer a member. Where Transnational Codes (see Section 3 in the Executive Summary) are concerned, the Commission must make the final decision, which if it overrules an ICO decision, may transgress the UK Government's "Brexit red lines", such as "putting UK citizens first" (House of Commons, 21 June 2017). The same difficulties complicate the accreditation of monitoring bodies by the ICO.

Data protection certification procedures and data protection seals and marks constitute voluntary schemes to evidence the existence of adequate safeguards in line with the accountability principles provided by the controller and processor. Additional binding and enforceable commitments through contractual or other legally binding instruments are expected (Article 42(2) GDPR). The competent Supervisory Authority or the EDPB shall issue the certification, which shall last no more than three years, subject to periodic reviews, and then come up for renewal. The EDPB in exercising its oversight role shall collate all certification mechanisms and seals and marks in a publicly available register (Article 42(8) GDPR). The EDPB may also adopt a common certification, the "European Data

Protection Seal" (Article 42(5)). As with Codes of conduct, the Supervisory Authorities must also accredit independent certification bodies for the issuing, periodic review and withdrawal of certifications (Article 43 GDPR).

Again, the ICO would have to work closely with the EDPB by reporting certification criteria and procedures, and the certifications and seals. At the same time, the Commission and EDPB must be able to place full reliance on the ICO to adopt adequate technical standards for the certification procedures, seals and marks in accordance with EU law. Article 55 [Competence] of the GDPR requires that the ICO must be "competent for the performance of the tasks assigned to and the exercise of the powers conferred on it in accordance with this Regulation"; however, this requires the ICO to fully align to EU regulations and EDPB guidances. As at June 2019 no information had been published by the ICO on the potential impact of Brexit on Codes of conduct (ICO – Codes of conduct) or certifications (ICO – Certification).

The EU would also have to endorse the ICO's competence for performance of these tasks (Article 55 GDPR) and to act as a lead national Supervisory Authority (Article 55), as well as to delegate to the ICO authorisation and advisory powers under the GDPR (Article 58(3) [Powers]) and trust its consistency (Article 63 [Consistency mechanism]). To enable all this will most likely require an agreement beyond a mere adequacy decision. As the UK will lose all input in the making of the foregoing EU instruments, data processing firms (including cloud service providers and data hosting-services) may come to consider the UK as an ineffective, relative "backwater" amongst the jurisdictions of choice (Harcourt, 2018).

4.1.3   Other safeguards

Binding Corporate Rules (BCR) in accordance with GDPR Article 47 enable international organisations and groups of organisations to make intra-organisational personal data transfers. BCRs have to be approved by a BCR Lead Supervisory Authority, which must take charge of coordinating it. The UK Government's No-deal Guidance recognises BCRs authorised before exit day (HM Government, 23 April 2019); however, the author does not consider BCRs to be a preferred post-Brexit solution for data transfers for the following reasons:

(1)   The application period is quite lengthy and therefore is not designed for the "mass market". The EU has developed a mutual recognition process under which one Member State is the "Lead Authority", but a straightforward application could still take 12 months to complete (ICO – Binding corporate rules). And the uptake of BCRs has been low: as at 25 May 2018, EU companies had obtained 131 authorisations from the EU, including 27 BCRs from the UK's ICO (European

Commission, 24 May 2018).

(2)   Post-Brexit, the ICO will play no more role in the BCR community, so BCRs will not be a viable option for UK-based companies for transferring data from the EU into the UK. The EDPB published a No-deal Brexit Information Note for organisations that have already selected the ICO as the BCR Lead Supervisory Authority, which clearly states that the ICO will no longer participate in the BCR community (EDPB, 12 February 2019b). Confusingly, the UK Government's No-deal Guidance presumes the ICO will continue to be able to authorise BCRs under domestic law (HM Government, 23 April 2019). This is open to interpretation, as the European Commission has currently an important role in BCR approvals. Companies whose BCRs are currently in the review stage with the ICO, or whose BCRs approving is pending at the EDPB, or who are already authorised BCR-holders, must identify a new BCR Lead Supervisory Authority according to the criteria laid down in Art. 29 WP263 (Art. 29 Data Protection WP, 11 April 2018).

(3)   BCRs are not as wide-ranging as adequacy decisions or an EU-UK data agreement, and they are too costly for small-and-medium sized enterprises (SMEs). Leading legal firms estimate that on average they will cost around £250,000 to set up (HM Government, 24 August 2018).

4.2   Derogations for specific purposes

In case of a non-adequacy decision (Chapter Three) or a lack of appropriate safeguards (Section 4.1), transfers of personal data to a third country or an international organisation may take place under terms and conditions pursuant to Article 49. These are presented in this Section and analysed for their relevance to post-Brexit Britain.

It is important to note that derogations for specific situations to provide a legal basis for data transfers are supposed to be only occasional, not usual, and should affect only a limited number of data subjects, and be necessary to the data subjects' compelling legitimate interests without compromising their interests or their rights. Derogations can be summarised under the following three categories:

(1)   **Explicit consent by the data subject** (Art. 49(1)(a))
Article 49(1)(a) GDPR provides a legal basis for data transfers if "the data subject has explicitly consented to the proposed transfer" after having been provided with all relevant information about the risks associated with such a transfer.

(2)   **Performance of the contract** (Art. 49(1)(b))
Article 49(1) GDPR gives data controllers legal grounds for data transfers if the data subject has approved such transfer in advance and (b) "the transfer is necessary for

the performance of a contract between the data subject and the controller", or (c) the transfer is "necessary for the performance of a contract concluded in the interest of the data subject between the controller and another natural of legal person".

(3) **Legitimate interest and other reasons** (Art. 49(1)(c-g))

Article 49(1) GDPR also provides a legal basis for data transfers when (d) the transfer is necessary for important reasons of public interest; (e) if it is necessary for the establishment, exercise, or defence of legal claims; (f) if "the transfer is necessary in order to protect the vital interests of the data subject [and] where the data subject is physically or legally incapable of giving consent"; or (g) if "the transfer is made from a register which according to Union or Member State law is intended to provide information to the public and which is open to consultation" under the strictures of EU law.

However, the scope of these alternatives for transfers to non-adequate countries and derogations from the provisions of the GDPR is more limited than that of an adequacy decision; in particular, the alternatives are vetted with Member State cooperation inside the EDPB (Article 70), from which the UK is excluding itself, so that it cannot influence their terms so as to help or strategically affect its own international trade negotiations.

PART III

The challenges: An "ambitious" agreement *vs.* the UK's bargaining power

The best move you can make in negotiation
is to think of an incentive the other person hasn't even thought of -
and then meet it.

– Eli Broad

Chapter 5

A POSSIBLE "AMBITIOUS" EU-UK DATA PROTECTION AGREEMENT: SCOPE AND REQUIREMENTS

In June 2018 the UK Government published a "technical note" summarising the benefits of a new EU-UK data protection agreement, – covering legal certainty, cooperation on enforcement and investigations, and efficiency savings for businesses and regulators working in collaboration with the EU (HM Government, 7 June 2018). This three-page "vision" foreran a more detailed white paper, on "The exchange and protection of personal data – a future partnership paper", which stresses the benefits of the UK's intent to build "a new, deep and special partnership with the EU" (Paragraph 22). It notes that the UK starts from "an unprecedented point of alignment with the EU" (Paragraph 4) and adoption of international data protection standards (Paragraphs 17 and 18), and proposes a UK-EU model for exchanging and protecting personal data (Paragraph 23) and for regulatory co-operation (Paragraphs 24-26) (HM Government, 24 August 2018).

This Chapter investigates how this vision evolved, analysing in particular what the UK can offer to collaboration in the areas of crime and terrorism prevention, and national security. It also reviews some critical requirements which the author identified as key to the European Commission's adequacy assessments, but which also must make part of any future EU-UK data protection agreement that might establish an even closer collaboration with the EU on data protection and the institutional set-up thereof. This includes safeguarding the rights of data subjects, establishing a redress mechanism, and adhering to the rulings of the ECHR and CJEU where EU data subjects are concerned. The analysis below will contribute to the assessment in the conclusions Section of how likely it is for the UK to obtain the international data protection agreement they desire.

5.1 The UK's bargaining power to shape a new relationship for data protection

The "Exiting the European Union" Select Committee of the House of Commons published a report on data flows and data protection after Brexit (House of Commons, Exiting the European Union Committee, 26 June 2018), which acknowledges the right of the European Commission to unilaterally decide the adequacy of the UK data regime. However, it proposes that a bilateral international agreement on data (*i.e.* a treaty) forms the basis of the future relationship (Paragraph 30).

Prime Minister May set it as an objective of the Brexit negotiations that the UK's Information Commissioner's Office should continue membership of the European Data Protection Board and participate in the EU's "one-stop shop" lead supervisory mechanism. May understood that the CJEU must continue to have jurisdiction over certain aspects of data protection after Brexit (Paragraph 31). The EU, however, to guard its decision-making autonomy, has so far not allowed any third country to sit on the EDPB. Even EEA countries like Norway are barred from the internal market of data (Paragraph 36). Prime Minister May proposed in her Florence Speech (PM Theresa May, 22 September 2017) and Munich Speech (PM Theresa May, 17 February 2018) that a close co-operation with EU agencies in the areas of security, criminal justice and law enforcement should continue after Brexit. The future partnership should include a continuation of EU-wide data sharing and cooperation between the UK and Europol and Eurojust (Paragraph 38). (HM Government, 18 September 2017). And in her Munich speech, PM May noted the "highly developed set of security and defence relationships: with the US and Five Eyes partners, with the Gulf and increasingly Asian partners too" (May, 2018[see Biblio for Munich Speech]). The UK has invested in critical capabilities beyond "world class special forces and intelligence services, which include a nuclear deterrent and two new aircraft carriers". Reading between the lines of these two speeches, the UK is using its sophisticated intelligence and security capabilities as bargaining chips. Although this Blue Paper focusses on the legal aspects of personal data transfer, political power plays will ultimately decide if the EU offers the UK a seat on the EDPB and close collaboration in the certification and Codes of Conduct schemes, the "one-stop shop", and maybe even a continuation with the EU's Binding Corporate Rules.

The UK vision of a future deep and special partnership was summarized by the UK negotiating team in three pillars:

(1)   an economic partnership transcending a Free Trade Agreement,

(2)   a security partnership for law enforcement and criminal justice, foreign security and defence; and

(3)   cross-cutting cooperative accords on matters such as data protection, science and innovation, *etc.* (HM Government, May 2018).

The author had access only to publicly available resources, not to classified recordings of senior public servants, ministers and heads of state. Sensitive negotiations involving national security take place behind closed doors. It may be inferred, however, that these are the UK's most valuable bargaining chips; notwithstanding that no precedents exist for "special treatment" of exiting EU Member States, the chips are so valuable that the UK just might be able to win a special relationship on data.

While the "Exiting the European Union" Select Committee report acknowledges the legal and negotiating challenges of such an international data protection agreement, it stresses its advantages for regulatory harmonisation and business certainty (Paragraph 47). The alternative legal processes herein analysed are considered by the Committee to be "unsatisfactory substitutes" that burden businesses with unnecessary bureaucracy (Paragraph 57). Therefore, to ensure continuity of data flows in both directions, an agreement over and above an adequacy decision is desirable. The reason is that the UK will have to establish its own adequacy mechanisms for third countries outside the EU, and in order to maintain adequacy with the EU, this will require co-operation with the EDPB and use of some of the alternative mechanisms contained in the GDPR (see also House of Commons, Exiting the European Union Select Committee (3 July 2018), "The progress of the UK's negotiations on EU withdrawal: Data", paragraph 51 of Select Committee Report).

The UK has rightly pointed out that it "is going beyond minimum EU requirements and will implement the GDPR and Law Enforcement Directive in full. Our Data Protection Act 2018 will provide a comprehensive and robust regulatory framework, compatible with the European Convention on Human Rights and Council of Europe Convention 108" (HM Government, May 2018:11). The UK has already accepted Title 7 of the Withdrawal Agreement (HM Government, 2018[Withdrawal Agreement, 21 November 2018]), providing assurances for the future to protect personal data already located in the UK, and has given assurances that the risk of gaps in the legal provisions for data transfers post-Brexit will be eliminated (House of Commons, 3 July 2018). They are naturally expecting something in return for all their efforts. Time is of the essence; the process for the UK to obtain an EU adequacy decision and to negotiate an EU-UK data protection agreement should be initiated as soon as possible.

5.2   Safeguarding the rights of data subjects

The transposition of the GDPR into national law in the Data Protection Act 2018, ch. 12 is the legal basis for safeguarding the rights of EU and UK residents and citizens. It covers the key provisions, including special personal data categories (Article 10-11 DPA 2018); the rights of data subjects (Article 12-14, 43-54 and 92-100); transfer of personal data to third countries (Article 18); the data protection principles (Article 34-42 and 85-91); security of data processing (Article 66, 107); data breach notification (Article 67-68, 108); and transfer of personal data to third countries (Article 72-78, 109). In addition, the DPA 2018 includes specific Codes of conduct for data sharing, direct marketing, age-appropriate design, and journalism (Article 121-124). The ICO has clearly stated, "The GDPR will still apply to any organisations in Europe who send you data, so you may need to help them decide how to transfer personal data to the UK in line with the GDPR" including the issue of consent. Moreover, companies will still need to comply with the "rights and obligations found in the GDPR" even in a No-deal scenario (ICO – Information rights and Brexit FAQs). The ICO intends to continue to work closely with European Supervisory Authorities to safeguard personal data.

5.3   Oversight and redress mechanisms

In a No-deal scenario without any EU-UK agreement, the UK's ICO could no longer partake in the GDPR's "one-stop shop" and the EDPB; therefore, the ICO would not be able to co-operate with EU supervising authorities to coordinate complaints from EU Member State citizens (House of Commons, Exiting the European Union Committee, 26 June 2018:paragraph 36). Indeed, a company that is established only in an EU Member State may be unable to report complaints to the ICO anymore. Although the ICO has said it wishes to maintain a strong relationship with the EDPB post-Brexit, it would lose its seat and vote therein. Even if some kind of withdrawal agreement or adequacy decision is made, the UK would still not be a Member during the transition period (House of Commons, Exiting the European Union Committee, 26 June 2018:paragraph 5, 36 and 37). Based on the policy papers reviewed previously, which evince the UK's hope for close cooperation between UK and EU regulators, including dispute resolution and non-compliance sanctions, redress for EU citizens should not be seen as an issue.

5.4   Adherence to rulings of the ECHR and CJEU

In the Chapter Two, the importance of the UK's participation in multilateral regimes to obtain a positive EU adequacy decision was highlighted. This will be an important factor, too, if the UK wishes to negotiate an EU-UK data protection agreement. It matters if the UK as a "third country" continues to be one of the 47 member states of the Council of Europe (CoE) along with all of the EU Member States (Council of Europe – "Chart of signatures and ratifications of Treaty 005"); thus, a signatory of the Convention for the Protection of Human Rights and Fundamental Freedoms of 4 November 1950, ETS No. 5 (*a.k.a.* the ECHR) and, consequently, subject to the jurisdiction of the European Court of

Human Rights (ECtHR), to which breaches of the Convention by member states may be appealed.

Yet some UK politicians have advocated that the UK should denounce the ECHR, because the jurisdiction of the ECtHR restricts Parliament's sovereignty in the manner of the CJEU (Boffey, 2018). PM May, in fact, was planning to put quitting the ECHR in her 2020 electoral manifesto. The Commission's view is that the UK should remain party to the ECHR, because it constitutes a privacy safeguard, but that in case the UK denounces the ECHR or fails to execute the ECtHR's judgments, a "guillotine clause" is needed in any bespoke EU-UK security partnership agreement, which would also impact the adequacy of the UK's data protection standards. This would mandate that the Commission's adequacy decision is withdrawn, or could be declared invalid by the CJEU (European Commission, 18 June 2018). If in future the UK should trigger such a "guillotine clause", it would nullify the UK-EU security partnership.

5.5   Conclusions: A future EU-UK data protection agreement

At the present time it is unclear what a special data protection agreement complementing or superseding an adequacy decision would look like, or whether there is any appetite in the EU for designing another customised, Privacy Shield-like agreement. It is also a question how far the EU would be willing to go in negotiating such an agreement. Although the UK Data Protection Act 2018 contains safeguards for the rights of data subjects, the role of the UK's Supervisory Authority, the ICO, in oversight and redress is weakened, not by the Act but by its post-Brexit exclusion from the one-stop shop mechanism and the EDPB. Even bigger concerns include the UK's data sharing agreement with the Five Eyes alliance, the surveillance practices and legal powers of the intelligence services, clashes over compliance with the ECtHR's judgments, and the exit of the UK from CJEU jurisdiction.

Data processing for law enforcement and intelligence gathering is governed by a different regime not entirely within EU jurisdiction at all. The UK will surely use its own law enforcement and intelligence data as a powerful bargaining chip in Brexit (and, given the new Johnson Government, post-Brexit) negotiations. One of the key conclusions of this Chapter is that the UK is planning to package its negotiations about the future relationship consisting of three pillars: an economic partnership, a security partnership, and cross-cutting accords that include data protection. This means that the future relationship is ideally to be negotiated as a package, such that data protection will not be treated in isolation. Furthermore, the UK has committed itself not only to "fully align" its data protection regime with EU law, but also maintain compatibility with the European Convention on Human Rights and the Council of Europe's Convention ETS No. 108 (HM Government, May

2018:11). One should note that this was the May Government's position; it may shift under PM Boris Johnson. Brexit negotiations are more than just technical discussions between subject-matter experts, they are political contests between players with conflicting motives.

The CJEU will always retain jurisdiction over companies controlling or processing personal data that are established in the EU, including the transfer of data in and out of the EU from and to the UK. This means that the UK has no prospect of setting up a "pirate harbour" (or "privacy sanctuary") for US tech companies trying to evade the privacy rights and data-subject rights of the Council of Europe or the European Union. The UK government would do well to tread on the opposite side of skirting EU law; even after it becomes free and clear of the CJEU's formal jurisdiction, both the European Commission and the CJEU – (even if one leaves the ECtHR out of account) – will continue to exert a powerful influence over the law and practice of data transfer into and out of the UK itself.

Chapter 6

CHALLENGES ARISING FROM THE PRACTICES OF UK LAW ENFORCEMENT AND INTELLIGENCE SERVICE

The UK's Data Protection Act 2018 provides in Part 4 [Law enforcement and intelligence services processing] and Section 110 [National security] a special regime for its own intelligence services.[9] It is important to mention that this is not part of the EU data protection framework; however, it is primarily about information and (personal) data sharing. The UK government considers that "National security is outside the scope of EU law [and] consequently, the processing of personal data for national security purposes is not within the scope of the GDPR" (HM Government, 25 May 2018). Law enforcement in the UK is covered by the UK's Investigatory Powers Act of 2016 (IPA), which comprehends all of the powers available to law enforcement and the security and intelligence agencies. This has become highly controversial, as this Chapter explains. The author believes that, despite the segregation of data protection from data processed for law enforcement and intelligence purposes, it is important to understand some of the latter issues, as this will impact the future data-relationship between the EU and UK.

6.1 Intelligence services and law enforcement: Data sharing and mass surveillance

Some EU Member States, and the public, especially, are highly critical of any form of intrusion into their privacy, particularly where intelligence agencies are involved. This public opinion should not be underestimated, as it will play a role when the UK's ongoing negotiations of its data-processing relationship with the EU. There are certain red lines it would be best not to cross, and ultimately these are not determined by governments and

---

9   National security exemptions were also provided in Section 28 and Schedule 11 of the DPA 1998.

their functionaries, but by the public.

The campaign to protect privacy and restrict (unregulated) data flows has its roots in recent history in certain parts of the EU, particularly in Germany, where revelations of widespread spying on Germans by the US National Security Agency in 2015 led to a more sceptical view of the Internet (Beattie, 2017). In 2010 UK Prime Minister David Cameron established the UK National Security Council (NSC), which was considered a revolutionary process that combined intelligence services, mixing officials from defence, foreign policy, cabinet ministries, and operations (Aldrich, 2015:400). Understandably, these enhanced powers have raised serious concerns. Privacy campaigners misgive the UK government's record of spying on its own citizens. The Five Eyes eavesdropping alliance, consisting of Australia, Canada, New Zealand, the US and the UK, has called on Internet providers and edge companies to help them spy on citizens. The concern is that this could involve exploiting the smartphones, search engines, and email of ordinary people, unbeknownst to them, intruding on their privacy even so far as to suck up data from their fitness trackers (Sayer, 2017).

In June 2017, 83 civil liberties organisations wrote to the government ministers responsible for the Five Eyes security community, demanding that they encourage and facilitate development of strong encryption of the communication systems, not their further weakening. The civil libertarians rejected engineering-in "backdoors" that deliberately weaken encryption software to give enforcement agencies easier access (Human Rights Watch, 2017).

Britain has data-sharing agreements with third countries, and EU and UK law enforcement agencies share data under separate agreements which cover terrorist financing, money laundering and other forms of financial crime (Thompson and Parker, 2017).

The UK Investigatory Powers Act 2016 has been dubbed "the Snooper's Charter" because it empowers UK security services to weaken encryption, to hack into private data, and to require ISPs to retain the browsing history of all users for 12 months.[10] The human rights campaigner organisation *Liberty* has challenged the government's power, in a High Court case, to command companies to store users' communication data, including Internet browsing history, and its right to access this personal data. *Liberty* Director Martha Spurrier stated, "Police and security agencies need tools to tackle serious crime in the digital age – but creating the most intrusive surveillance regime of any democracy in the world is unlawful, unnecessary and ineffective" (Liberty, 27 April 2018). The Court ruled that ministers cannot issue data retention orders without independent authorisation and review, or for reasons

---

[10] The IPA is accompanied by a number of technical provisions, which include the Investigations Powers (Codes of Practice and Miscellaneous Amendments); Investigatory Powers (Technical Capability) Regulations; Investigatory Powers (Review of Notices and Technical Advisory Board) Regulations; Investigatory Powers (Disclosure of Statistical Information) Regulations; and Investigatory Powers (Interception by Businesses *etc.* for Monitoring and Record-keeping Purposes) Regulations.

unrelated to the investigation of serious crime. At the hearing Lord Justice Singh concluded, "Part 4 of the Investigatory Powers Act 2016 is incompatible with the fundamental rights in EU law" (*Justice v. Home Office* [2018] EWHC 975 (Admin)). The High Court ordered the amendment by 1 November 2018 of the secondary legislation that had been implemented in and through the Data Retention and Acquisition Regulations 2018, to raise the threshold such that accessing "communications data" may be done only for the purpose of investigating serious crime, and only after receiving prior approval by an independent Investigatory Powers Commissioner (The Data Retention and Acquisition Regulations 2018 (No. 1123)).

Shortly after this judgment, the Investigatory Powers Tribunal, an independent court set up to pass judgment on the lawfulness of intrusion into privacy by public bodies, concluded that the Foreign Office had repeatedly broken the law for more than 15 years by allowing the GCHQ, the UK's electronic surveillance agency, to hoard data on British citizens, giving them *carte blanche* to demand data from telecoms and internet companies (Archer, 2018).

Liberty together with Amnesty International, Privacy International, and eleven other human right groups won another, joined case before the European Court of Human Rights (ECtHR), which reviewed the secret surveillance schemes of UK government agencies and the wider UK legal framework for interception of communications and intelligence sharing. The ECHR ruled that the UK law establishing a regime for mass surveillance and historical bulk interception violated the right to private life protected by Article 8, and the right to freedom of expression protected by Article 10 of the European Convention on Human Rights (*Big Brother Watch and Others v. the United Kingdom* (Merits and Just Satisfaction)); see also "Some aspects of UK surveillance regimes violate Convention", press release ECHR 299 (2018) ECHR Judgement (2018a and b). It concluded that the interception of communications data is a serious breach of privacy and that the UK's regime for authorising bulk interception was incapable of keeping the "interference with private life" to what is "necessary in a democratic society", and that it is "disproportionate to the objective pursued" (Liberty, 13 September 2018).

In a second challenge at the High Court, Liberty won the right to proceed with its challenge of the IPA and its empowerment of state agencies to collect "internet usage in bulk and without individualised suspicion" (Liberty, 29 November 2018). In June 2019 the UK's Investigatory Powers Commissioner's Office (IPCO), which safeguards privacy protections, stated after an investigation that MI5 had breached data-handling obligations under the IPA. The Commissioner concluded that the way MI5 had been holding and handling personal data was "undoubtedly unlawful" and "is currently, in effect, in 'special measures' and the historical lack of compliance [...] is of such gravity that IPCO will need to be satisfied to a greater degree than usual that it is 'fit for purpose'" (Liberty, 11 June 2019).

The European Commission's concerns in recognising that the UK might not meet the adequate data protection standards and safeguards for reciprocal agreements, in particular certain provisions in the Investigatory Powers Act 2016, and relating the collection and storage of personal data by security services has been identified (House of Lords, 22 March 2017:paragraph 159), but no specific action to address these concerns has been taken yet.

Considering these stark warnings from courts, tribunals and watchdogs, the UK's individual and mass surveillance regime risks compromising the EU's requirements. In 2013 it was estimated that the UK's intelligence service (GCHQ), assisted by the NSA, intercepted most of the fibre-optic communications cables going in and out of the UK. Information about the companies that assist with this are classified top secret; however, an article in the *Guardian* suggested that GCHQ was harvesting a quarter of all high-capacity cable traffic, and was probing 21.6 petabytes of information a day, which is equivalent to 192 times the British Library's entire book collection (MacAskill, Hopkins et al (21 June 2013)). As much of the world's email traffic is routed through the US; thus, it can be expected that a great deal of it is being monitored by the GCHQ and NSA.

Although surveillance and data gathering by intelligence services is not currently regulated by EU law, the UK as part of the Five Eyes arrangement has become notorious as conducting more unconsented surveillance than most, maybe all other EU Member States. In future, the UK may be challenged not only by civil right groups in UK courts, but also by the EU and its Member States in a way that Brexit cannot circumvent. Mass surveillance clearly violates any attempt at purpose-limitation. Criticism of mass surveillance in China also bids fair to spill over onto the UK, as the EU is increasingly critical of the risks of Big Data and its entanglement with the deep state.

6.2   Exemptions from the GDPR: Access to the personal data of EU citizens

The DPA 2018, Schedule 2 [Exemptions from the GDPR], Part 1(4) [Immigration] exempts the UK government from conceding to individual rights requests "that would undermine the maintenance of effective immigration control". Leigh Day, the law firm that represents the3*million*, a non-profit organisations which is acting on behalf of EU citizens in the UK, argues that the Home Office post-Brexit could deny EU citizens access to their personal records when applying for settled status. The court heard that the Windrush immigration scandal showed that data was often inaccurate, and the Joint Council for the Welfare of Immigrants, the Law Society, and the Bar Council opposed such an exemption in the Data Protection Act 2018 (Schedule 2 [Exemptions from the GDPR], Paragraph 4) introduced by the Home Office (Bowcott, 2019). This is also the view of the House of Commons Home Affairs Committee, which is unconvinced that all those involved in the Brexit negotiations fully understand the implications of access to data (Paragraph 6), and which also suggested that the immigration exemption in the Data Protection Act "could undermine a data adequacy decision" (House of Commons, 9 October 2018:paragraph 7).

Barring access to one's own personal records kept by public bodies would also violate the EU Charter of Fundamental Rights (European Union, 18 December 2000), Article 8 of which grants the data subject the right of access to data that has been collected about him or her, plus the right of the data subject to require any errors therein to be rectified. The May Government has determined that the Charter will not be retained post-Brexit in the body of EU law enacted into UK law under the terms of the European Union (Withdrawal) Act 2018 (House of Lords, 11 July 2018:46, paragraph 144); however, denying such a fundamental right weakens the UK's negotiating position in a proceeding to reach a data agreement or obtain an adequacy decision.

6.3   Misuse of Artificial Intelligence

The rise of new technical capabilities like artificial intelligence (AI) and data analytics has introduced powerful, systematic methods of identification, profiling and biometric recognition, such as facial recognition, recognition of emotions in images of faces and in speech, identification of data subjects' age, gender and ethnicity.   Fifty-two experts appointed to the EU's High-Level Expert Group on Artificial Intelligence (AI HLEG), comprising representatives from academia, civil society, and industries, have expressed concerns about the potential "to build up a China-style high-tech surveillance state".   In June 2019 the expert panel reported out some stark warnings against the use of AI to control and monitor citizens (Delcker, 2019).   The document made 33 recommendations to EU policy makers, calling on them to "ban AI-enabled mass scale scoring of individuals" and for "very clear and strict rules for surveillance for national security purposes and other purposes claimed to be in the public or national interest".   It also called on Member State governments to "refrain from disproportionate and mass surveillance of individuals" (AI HLEG, 2019).

Although the experts' recommendations are non-binding, they are expected to influence policy decisions by the European Commission.   This could lead to a clearer definition of the "red lines" beyond which Member State governments should not pass; which applications should be banned to what extent; but also how AI could be used beneficially in the future.   If in future the UK should transgress any "red lines" which the EU should have legislated, this could compromise or cause the withdrawal even of an adequacy decision already rendered.

The UK is among the countries in the world with the largest number of CCTV cameras installed in public places. The British Security Industry Association (BSIA) estimates that the UK had between 4 and 5.9 million such cameras in 2015. The UK government's Surveillance Camera Commissioner[11] Tony Porter questioned why "[w]e have millions of cameras in this country and Europeans look at us askance that our society actually accepts the volume of cameras we do" (BBC, 2015). It is also estimated that there are half a million CCTV surveillance cameras in London alone, 15,516 of which are just in the metropolitan Underground (Caught on Camera website). In his Annual Report 2017/18 the Surveillance Camera Commissioner stressed that "new standards and guidance is needed to cover the operations and use of more advanced technologies such as automatic facial recognition and video analytics" (Surveillance Camera Commissioner, 2019). The report also stressed that the Data Protection Act 2018 provides "strong powers to protect against data processing abuse"; however, "it does not provide a holistic approach to regulating the actual use of surveillance" (Surveillance Camera Commissioner, 2019:5).

The House of Lords Select Committee on Artificial Intelligence identified some benefits, but also many challenges coming from technological changes and their impact on society, including public trust in the use of personal data, the ethics of data sharing between organisations, bias in data, monopolisation of versus equal access to data, automated decision making and its consequences such as decisional errors. The report makes recommendations to mitigate risks and proposes alternative mechanisms for industry self-regulation. The picture that emerges is one where technology explodes, but society's ability to manage its benefits and control its untoward consequences lags behind (House of Lords, 16 April 2018). The UK government has tried various approaches to these issues, one being a consultation over a new *Data Science Ethical Framework* structured around seven "key principles" for guiding the work of data scientists (HM Government, 13 June 2018); however, after its launch in July 2017, the initial Framework was withdrawn due to notable criticism (Fishenden, 2017; HM Government, 19 May 2016). And this is just one example of many attempts that have been made to control or at least moderate the impact of AI, and a clear indication of how difficult it will be to regulate it.

6.4 Consequences of the UK losing access to EU data and intelligence

The House of Lords' European Union Committee published a report "Brexit: the proposed UK-EU security treaty" (House of Lords, 11 July 2018) outlining the Government's position in regards to collaboration with EU Member States in the field of security and intelligence

---

[11] The Surveillance Camera Commissioner's website is available at
https://www.gov.uk/government/organisations/surveillance-camera-commissioner (accessed August 2019).

sharing. It broaches the potential consequences that a breakdown of the data-relationship with the EU could have. It focusses on future security cooperation and warns of the consequences of getting locked out of EU law enforcement databases; including the following agreements and their restrictions on data access to key information systems:

(1)   **the European Arrest Warrant (EAW) and its Information System**

This legal framework facilitates extradition of individuals between EU Member States for prosecution or to serve a prison sentence for an existing conviction. As per the House of Lords report, it is unlikely that the UK will have the same access-level as an EU Member State post-Brexit. It has been suggested to fall back on the 1957 Council of Europe Convention on Extradition which, however, could lead to delays, higher costs, and potential political interference.

(2)   **police and security cooperation and systems**

There are a number of agencies and resources to which the UK had full access as an EU Member State. These included national security agencies and border control access to the:

(i)   Second Generation Schengen Information System (SIS II), which alerts to individuals of interest to EU law enforcement agencies;

(ii)   the European Criminal Records Information System (ECRIS), a secure electronic system for exchanging information between Member States on criminal convictions.

(iii) Passenger Name Records (PNR), which enforces the Passenger Name Record Directive mandating collection of information by air carriers as part of the booking process;

(iv)   the European Asylum Dactyloscopy Database (Eurodac), and

(v)   the Prüm Framework, which allows searches for DNA profiles, fingerprints and vehicle registration information in other Member States' databases;

(3)   **specialised agencies fighting terrorism, cybercrime and other serious forms of organised crime**, including:

(i)   Europol, which supports law enforcement agencies by providing access to intelligence from other EU Member States and from the Europol Information System (EIS), which pools information on criminals and terrorists from across the EU;

(ii)   Eurojust, the agency tasked to support and strengthen coordination between Member States' investigation and prosecution authorities;

(iii) EU Justice and Home Affairs databases (House of Commons, 9 October 2018).

Reports compiled by the House of Lords and House of Commons consistently conclude that co-operation between the UK and EU Member States is "mission-critical" for UK law enforcement agencies (House of Lords, December 2016). Due to its significant operational dependence on EU systems and databases, the UK Government opted into the proposed Regulation on "interoperability between EU information systems" (House of Lords, 11 July 2018).

It should be noted that sharing information between law enforcement and intelligence agencies has been put outside the scope of the EU privacy framework (GDPR); however, it will be an important consideration when the UK negotiates its EU-UK data protection agreement or needs to make concessions for an adequacy decision. One may expect a lot of common interests to be shared by both sides, and the UK is likely to seek a very close legal and regulatory alignment, anyway, which will go beyond information sharing for law enforcement and intelligence purposes.

Chapter 7

CONCLUSIONS

⟨⟨ℜ⟩⟩

If the UK keeps its legal and regulatory data protection framework aligned to the GDPR and actually enforces compliance through the ICO, then the European Commission should assess the UK data regime to be adequate. This should be the UK's first priority and not a "bargaining chip". The ICO's recent record of fines shows that it wants to be seen as a strong regulator enforcing the GDPR; however, the problem is that an adequacy assessment and decision might take several years regardless, and is likely to be bargained over in future trade negotiations.

A further complication is the European Commission's lack of transparency about how past adequacy decisions have been made. As analysed in Chapter Three, some guidance is available, but as witness the latest adequacy decision concerning Japan, decisions can be politically motivated, and the latest ones have been forged with the aim of facilitating trade agreements. All this may cause continuing uncertainty and higher costs for business, which may in response either move its data processing or even its business entirely to the Single Market. There is strong evidence that an exodus of (personal) data from the UK to counties such as Ireland and the Netherlands has started already (see Section 3.4).

European concepts of legal proportionality have been taken into UK common law and now entered into precedential thinking. These concepts will continue to be relied on after Brexit. It is understood that the CJEU has no jurisdiction over the UK any more, which is bound to lead to conflicts of law. This introduces some risk over obtaining, and maintaining an adequacy decision, as this will be a subject of regular review by the European Commission (GDPR, Art. 45(3)).

An adequacy decision, even if granted relatively quickly, is not in itself the Holy Grail. The UK still must negotiate data-transfer agreements with third countries, which will also fall within the scope of future trade agreements. As many of these countries have not yet obtained (and might never obtain) adequacy status from the Commission, they may or may not to meet the adequacy requirements of either EU nor UK law, now or in the future. Other mechanisms are therefore needed (see Chapter Four). Most of these mechanisms require close cooperation with the EDPB. A special EU-UK data protection agreement or mutual adequacy decision should be preferred over a mere adequacy decision for itself only, as this would maintain some ICO influence at EU-level, and better position the UK to solve the problems of international third-country data transfers. For the reasons detailed in this Blue Paper, the UK is unlikely to be able to reach such an agreement.

Notwithstanding all the reasons that speak against an ambitious data protection agreement, as a special data protection agreement would not be limited to the private sector, it is sometimes alleged that the UK holds certain "bargaining chips". The prospect of data from UK intelligence services and law enforcement agencies, in particular information obtained through the Five Eyes agreement, being shared might interest certain EU Member States. This might be the incentive for negotiating something more substantial than an adequacy decision. The EU is aware of the UK's global reach and influence, and might be willing to make some concessions in exchange, such as giving the ICO special status on the EDPB. This would depend critically on the EU and its member states trusting the UK, that all of the intelligence information it might feed them would never be "one-sided", or even disinformation.

The worst-case scenario – from a data protection and human rights perspective – would be if the UK should "race to the bottom" of data-protection standards, to attract inward investment by Big Data exploiters and/or to pursue easy trade agreements with third counties at the expense of data protection. In such a scenario, the UK would essentially forfeit its adequacy status under EU law. This would bear serious (and time- and money-costly) consequences for businesses, which would be obliged to turn to alternative mechanisms for protected data transfer that could be implemented without government cooperation, as presented in this Blue Paper.

It has been widely acknowledged that Data is the "steam" and the "oil" of the digital economy. Data has fundamental value, but needs to be accessible and "transported" between organisations and countries without significant delays to realise this value. Brexit could lead to additional costs, bureaucratic inefficiencies, and/or delays in data flows between the EU and UK. This would have negative consequences for the economy, but also for national security. This Paper has shown that certain legal options exist that could mitigate these concerns; however, to avoid any chaos for the stakeholders involved, UK legislators and regulators should not leave this to the last minute, but initiate now the actions recommended above.

BIBLIOGRAPHY

BIBLIOGRAPHY

Literature

AI HLEG (26 June 2019) "Policy and Investment Recommendations for Trustworthy AI", European Commission. Available at https://ec.europa.eu/digital-single-market/en/high-level-expert-group-artificial-intelligence (accessed August 2019).

Aldrich, Richard (2 March 2015) "The 100 billion dollar brain: central intelligence machinery in the UK and the US", *International Affairs*, Volume 91, pages 393-403.

APEC Privacy Framework (2017), Asia-Pacific Economic Cooperation, CTI Sub-Fora & Industry Dialogues Groups, Electronic Commerce Steering Group (ECSG), APEC Secretariat (Singapore). Available at https://www.apec.org/Publications/2017/08/APEC-Privacy-Framework-(2015) (accessed July 2019).

Archer, Joseph (24 July 2018) "GCHQ's licence to snoop on citizens was 'unlawful' for more than a decade", *The Telegraph*, Technology Intelligence.

Art. 29 Data Protection Working Party (11 April 2018) "Working Document Setting Forth a Co-Operation Procedure for the approval of 'Binding Corporate Rules' for controllers and processors under the GDPR", WP263 rev.01, adopted by the EDPB.

Art. 29 Data Protection Working Party (11 April 2018) "Working document 01/2014 on Draft Ad hoc contractual clauses 'EU data processor to non-EU sub-processor'", WP214, 747/14/EN.

Art. 29 Data Protection Working Party (28 Nov 2017) "EU – U.S. Privacy Shield – First annual Joint Review", WP 255.

Art. 29 Data Protection Working Party (13 April 2016) "Opinion 01/2016 on the EU-U.S. Privacy Shield draft adequacy decision", WP 238.

Art. 29 Data Protection Working Party – Opinions and recommendations. Available at https://ec.europa.eu/justice/article-29/documentation/opinion-recommendation/index_en.htm (accessed February 2019).

Baker, Jennifer (30 October 2018) "What does the newly signed 'Convention 108+' mean for UK adequacy?", IAPP (International Association of Privacy Professionals). Available at https://iapp.org/news/a/what-does-the-newly-signed-convention-108-mean-for-uk-adequacy/ (accessed May 2018).

BBC (26 January 2015) "CCTV: Too many cameras useless, warns surveillance watchdog Tony Porter". Available at https://www.bbc.co.uk/news/uk-30978995 (accessed August 2019).

Beattie, Alan (4 Dec 2017) "EU trade data flows are becoming the new GMOs", FT.com.

Boffey, Daniel (18 June 2018) "Brussels seeks to tie UK to European human rights court after Brexit", *The Guardian*.

Bowcott, Owen (17 Jan 2019) "Data laws could harm EU citizens' attempts to stay in UK, court told: Judge grants hearing of judicial review request after being told millions cannot access records", *The Guardian*.

Brinded, Lianna (1 April 2017) "There's a widely touted fact that Brexiteers misuse when it comes to Brexit talks", *Business Insider*. Available at https://www.businessinsider.com.au/berenberg-eu-has-greater-bargaining-power-than-uk-in-brexit-talks-2017-3 (accessed July 2019).

Buttarelli, Giovanni (May 2016) "The EU GDPR is a clarion call for a new digital gold standard", *International Data Privacy Law*, Volume 6, Issue 2, pp. 77-78.

Bygrave, Lee Andrew (2014) *Data Privacy Law: An International Perspective* (Oxford University Press, Oxford.

Caught on Camera website at https://www.caughtoncamera.net/news/how-many-cctv-cameras-in-london/ (accessed August 2019).

Council of Europe (28 January 1981) "Convention for the Protection of Individuals with regard to Automatic Processing of Personal Data (Convention 108)", ETS No. 108.

Council of Europe (4 November 1950) "Convention for the Protection of Human Rights and Fundamental Freedoms", Rome.

Council of Europe – "Chart of signatures and ratifications of Treaty 223: Protocol amending the Convention for the Protection of Individuals with regard to Automatic Processing of Personal Data". Available at https://www.coe.int/en/web/conventions/full-list/-/conventions/treaty/223/signatures (accessed June 2019).

Council of Europe – "Chart of signatures and ratifications of Treaty 108". Available at https://www.coe.int/en/web/conventions/full-list/-/conventions/treaty/108/signatures (accessed May 2019).

Council of Europe – "Chart of signatures and ratifications of Treaty 005". Available at https://www.coe.int/en/web/conventions/full-list/-/conventions/treaty/005/signatures?p_auth=fh9uaCcK (accessed May 2019).

Council of Europe – European Treaty Series (ETS), the "Complete list of the Council of Europe's treaties". Available at https://www.coe.int/en/web/conventions/full-list (accessed May 2019).

CJEU (6 October 2015) *Maximilian Schrems v. Data Protection Commissioner*, Case C-362/14. ECLI:EU:C:2015:6506, Judgment of 6 October 2015.

Conservative Home – Brexit, "Theresa May's speech on Brexit: full text" (April 25, 2016). Available at https://www.conservativehome.com/parliament/2016/04/theresa-mays-speech-on-brexit-full-text.html (accessed August 2019).

Data Protection Act 2018 c. 12.

Data Protection Act 1998 c. 29.

Data Retention and Acquisition Regulations 2018 (No. 1123), statutory instrument, 31st October 2018.

Data Protection Network (September 2018) "Brexit, GDPR and Data Protection: What happens if the UK becomes a third country?".

Delcker, Janosch (24 June 2019) "AI experts call to curb mass surveillance: The EU's top AI experts say regulation should focus on high-risk applications", *Politico*.

Delegation of the European Union to Japan (23/01/2019) "EU-Japan Economic Partnership Agreement (EPA)". Available at https://eeas.europa.eu/delegations/japan_en/56981 (accessed June 2019).

ECHR (13 September 2018b) "Some aspects of UK surveillance regimes violate Convention", Press Release ECHR 299(2018).

ECHR Judgement (13 September 2018b) – Cases can be reviewed on the ECHR database. Available at https://hudoc.echr.coe.int (accessed May 2019).

EDPB (12 February 2019) "Information note on data transfers under the GDPR in the event of a no-deal Brexit".

EDPB (4 June 2019) "Guidelines 1/2019 on Codes of Conduct and Monitoring Bodies under Regulation 2016/679", version 2, adopted.

EDPB (4 June 2019) "Guidelines 4/2018 on the accreditation of certification bodies under Article 43 of the General Data Protection Regulation (2016/679) - Annex 1", version 3, adopted.

EDPB (4 June 2019) "Guidelines 1/2018 on certification and identifying certification criteria in accordance with Articles 42 and 43 of the Regulation 2016/679 - Annex 2", version 3, adopted.

ECHR Judgement – Grand Chamber Panel's decision (4 February 2019) "Big Brother Watch and Others v. the United Kingdom", applications nos. 58170/13, 62322/14 and 24960/15; ECHR 053 (2019).

ECHR Judgement (13 September 2018a) "Case of Big Brother Watch and others v. The United Kingdom (Merits and Just Satisfaction)", applications nos. 58170/13, 62322/14 and 24960/15, Judgment 13.9.2018 [Section I]; Strasbourg).

ECHR (13 September 2018b) "Some aspects of UK surveillance regimes violate Convention", press release ECHR 299(2018).

ECHR Judgement (4 Dec 2015) "Case of Roman Zakharov v. Russia", Application no. 47143/06, Strasbourg.

ECHR Judgement (29 April 2014) "Case of L.H. v. Latvia", Application no. 52019/07, Strasbourg.

ECHR Judgement (2 August 1984) "Malone v. United Kingdom", 8691/79 7 EHRR 10, Strasbourg.

ECHR Judgement (6 September 1978) "Case of Klass and others v. Germany", Application no. 5029/71, Strasbourg.

EDPB (12 February 2019) "Information note on data transfers under the GDPR in the event of a no-deal Brexit".

EDPB (12 February 2019b) "Information note on BCRs for companies which have ICO as BCR Lead Supervisory Authority".

EDPB - View all our documents by Publication Types. Available at https://edpb.europa.eu/our-work-tools/our-documents_en (accessed June 2019).

EDPB – GDPR Guidelines, Recommendations and Best Practices. Available at https://edpb.europa.eu/our-work-tools/general-guidance/gdpr-guidelines-recommendations-best-practices_en (accessed March 2019).

EDPS (30 May 2016) "Opinion on the EU-US Privacy Shield Draft Adequacy Decision", Opinion 4/2016.

European Union (18 December 2000) "Charter of Fundamental Rights of the European Union", 2000/C 364/01, OJEC C264, European Parliament, the Council and the Commission.

European Union Agency for Fundamental Rights – EU Charter of Fundamental Rights. Available at https://fra.europa.eu/en/charterpedia/article/8-protection-personal-data (accessed March 2019).

European Commission (23 Jan 2019) "European Commission adopts adequacy decision on Japan, creating the world's largest area of safe data flows", press release, IP/19/421 (Brussels).

European Commission and PPC (23 January 2019) "Joint Statement by Haruhi Kumazawa, Commissioner of the Personal Information Protection Commission (PPC) of Japan and Věra Jourová, Commissioner for Justice, Consumers and Gender Equality of the European Commission").

European Commission (19 December 2018) COM (2018)860 final "Report from the Commission to the European Parliament and the Council on the second annual review of the functioning of the EU-US Privacy Shield".

European Commission (17 July 2018) "The European Union and Japan agreed to create the world's largest area of safe data flows", press release, IP/18/4501 (Tokyo).

European Commission (12 July 2016) Commission Implementing Decision 2016/1250

"Pursuant to Directive 95/46/EC on the Adequacy of the Protection Provided by the EU-US Privacy Shield", 2016 O.J. (L 207) 1.

European Commission (18 June 2018) "Framework for the future relationship: Police & judicial cooperation in criminal matters", Task Force for the Preparation and Conduct of the Negotiations with the United Kingdom under Article 50 (TEUTF50)).

European Commission (24 May 2018) – List of companies for which the EU BCR cooperation procedure is closed. Available at https://ec.europa.eu/info/law/law-topic/data-protection/international-dimension-data-protection/binding-corporate-rules-bcr_en#listofcompanies (accessed May 2019).

European Commission (12 July 2016) "European Commission launches EU-U.S. Privacy Shield: stronger protection for transatlantic data flows", press release, IP/16/2461, Brussels.

European Commission COM(2015)497 final (14 October 2015) "Trade for All: Towards a more responsible trade and investment policy".

European Commission Decision (2010/87/EU) of 5 February 2010 "on standard contractual clauses for the transfer of personal data to processors established in third countries under Directive 95/46/EC", notified under document C(2010) 593)) [EU Controller to non-EU or EEA processor]".

European Commission Decision (2004/915/EC) of 27 December 2004 "amending Decision (2001/497/EC) as regards the introduction of an alternative set of standard contractual clauses for the transfer of personal data to third countries [EU Controller to non-EU or EEA controller]", notified under document number C(2004) 5271)).

European Commission Decision (2001/497/EC) of 15 June 2001 "on standard contractual clauses for the transfer of personal data to third countries, under Directive 95/46/EC, notified under document number C(2001) 1539) [EU Controller to non-EU or EEA controller]".

European Commission [Adequacy Decision – Andorra] (19 October 2010) Decision (2010/625/EU) "pursuant to Directive 95/46/EC on the adequate protection of personal data in Andorra", notified under C(2010) 7084.

European Commission [Adequacy Decision – Argentina] (30 June 2003) Decision (2003/190/EC) "pursuant to Directive 95/46/EC on the adequate protection of personal data in Argentina".

European Commission [Adequacy Decision – Canada (commercial organisations)] (20 December 2001) Decision "pursuant to Directive 95/46/EC on the adequate protection of personal data provided by the Canadian Personal Information Protection and Electronic Documents Act", notified under document C(2001) 4539.

European Commission [Adequacy Decision – Faroe Islands] (5 March 2010): Decision (2010/146/EU) "pursuant to Directive 95/46/EC on the adequate protection provided by the Faeroese Act on processing of personal data", notified under document C(2010) 1130.

European Commission [Adequacy Decision – Guernsey] (21 November 2003) Decision (2003/821/EC) "on the adequate protection of personal data in Guernsey", notified under document number C(2003) 4309.

European Commission [Adequacy Decision – Israel] (31 January 2011) Decision (2011/61/EC) "pursuant to Directive 95/46/EC on the adequate protection of personal data by the State of Israel with regard to automated processing of personal data", notified under document C(2011) 332.

European Commission [Adequacy Decision – Isle of Man] (28 April 2004) Decision (2004/411/EC) "on the adequate protection of personal data in the Isle of Man".

European Commission [Adequacy Decision – Japan] (23 January 2019) Implementing Decision (2019/419/EU) "pursuant to Regulation (EU) 2016/679 on the adequate protection of personal data by Japan under the Act on the Protection of Personal Information.

European Commission [Adequacy Decision – Jersey] (8 May 2008) Commission Decision (2008/393/EC) "pursuant to Directive 95/46/EC on the adequate protection of personal data in Jersey", notified under document number C(2008) 1746.

European Commission [Adequacy Decision – New Zealand] (19 December 2012) Implementing Decision (2013/65/EU) "pursuant to Directive 95/46/EC on the adequate protection of personal data by New Zealand", notified under document C(2012) 9557.

European Commission [Adequacy Decision – Switzerland] (26 July 2000) Decision (2000/518/EC) pursuant to Directive 95/46/EC on the adequate protection of personal data provided in Switzerland", notified under document number C(2000) 2304.

European Commission [Adequacy Decision – Uruguay] (21 August 2012) Decision (2012/484/EU) "pursuant to Directive (95/46/EC) on the adequate protection of personal data by the Eastern Republic of Uruguay with regard to automated processing of personal data", notified under C(2012) 5704.

European Commission [Adequacy Decision – USA (limited to the Privacy Shield)] (12 July 2016) Implementing Decision (2016/1250/EU) "pursuant to Directive 95/46/EC on the adequacy of the protection provided by the EU-U.S. Privacy Shield", notified under document C(2016) 4176.

European Commission – Adequacy Decisions "How the EU determines if a non-EU country has an adequate level of data protection.". Available at https://ec.europa.eu/info/law/law-topic/data-protection/international-dimension-data-protection/adequacy-decisions_en (accessed May 2019).

European Commission Data Protection Law [Enforcement] Directive EU 2016/680 (27 April 2016) "on the protection of natural persons with regard to the processing of personal data by competent authorities for the purposes of the prevention, investigation, detection or prosecution of criminal offences or the execution of criminal penalties, and on the free movement of such data, and repealing Council Framework Decision 2008/977/JHA".

European Commission Directive 2002/58/EC (12 July 2002) "concerning the processing of personal data and the protection of privacy in the electronic communications sector (Directive on privacy and electronic communications)".

European Commission Directive 95/46/EC (24 October 1995) "on the protection of individuals with regard to the processing of personal data and on the free movement of such data [EU Data Protection Directive]".

European Commission Regulation (EU) 2018/1807 (14 November 2018) "on a framework for the free flow of non-personal data in the European Union", OJ L 303.

European Commission Regulation 2018/1725 (23 October 2018) "on the protection of natural persons with regard to the processing of personal data by the Union institutions, bodies, offices and agencies and on the free movement of such data, and repealing Regulation (EC) No 45/2001 and Decision No 1247/2002/EC".

European Commission Regulation (EU) 2016/679 (27 April 2016) "on the protection of natural persons with regard to the processing of personal data and on the free movement of such data, and repealing Directive 95/46/EC (General Data Protection Regulation)".

European Commission Regulation (EU) No 182/2011 (16 February 2011) "laying down the rules and general principles concerning mechanisms for control by Member States of the Commission's exercise of implementing powers".

European Parliament Resolution of 5 July 2018 "on the adequacy of the protection afforded by the EU-US Privacy Shield (2018/2645(RSP)", P8_TA-PROV(2018)0315.

European Commission – Adequacy decisions. "How the EU determines if a non-EU country has an adequate level of data protection." Available at https://ec.europa.eu/info/law/law-topic/data-protection/international-dimension-data-protection/adequacy-decisions_en (accessed May 2019).

European Commission – Data Protection. Available at https://ec.europa.eu/info/law/law-topic/data-protection_en (accessed May 2019).

European Commission – EU-Japan. "EU-Japan Economic Partnership Agreement". Available at https://ec.europa.eu/trade/policy/in-focus/eu-japan-economic-partnership-agreement (accessed February 2019).

European Commission – EU-US data transfers. "How personal data transferred between the EU and US is protected", Commercial sector: EU-US Privacy Shield. Available at https://ec.europa.eu/info/law/law-topic/data-protection/international-dimension-data-protection/eu-us-data-transfers_en (accessed March 2019).

European Commission – Standard Contractual Clauses (SCC). Available at https://ec.europa.eu/info/law/law-topic/data-protection/international-dimension-data-protection/standard-contractual-clauses-scc_en (accessed January 2019).

European Council Decision 2019/682 (9 April 2019) "authorising Member States to ratify, in the interest of the European Union, the Protocol amending the Council of Europe Convention for the Protection of Individuals with regard to Automatic Processing of Personal Data", 2 May 2019 L115/7.

European Parliament (August 2018) "The future EU-UK relationship: options in the field of the protection of personal data for general processing activities and for processing for law enforcement purposes", study requested by the LIBE committee, Directorate General for Internal Policies of the Union, Policy Department for Citizens' Rights and Constitutional Affairs, Civil Liberties, Justice and Home Affairs (Brussels).

European Parliament Resolution of 5 July 2018"on the adequacy of the protection afforded by the EU-US Privacy Shield (2018/2645(RSP)", P8_TA-PROV(2018)0315.

European Union Agency for Fundamental Rights (FRA), European Court of Human Rights, Council of Europe and European Data Protection Supervisor (EDPS) (2018) Handbook on European data protection law, (Luxembourg: Publications Office of the European Union). Available at http://fra.europa.eu/en/publication/2018/handbook-european-data-protection-law (October 2018).

European Union (Withdrawal) Act 2019 ch. 16, 26 June 2018.

Financial Times (13 Sep 2018) "No-deal Brexit: FT assesses government impact papers", FT.com.

Fishenden, Jerry (5 July 2017) "Improving data science ethics: New tech observations from the UK". Available at https://ntouk.wordpress.com/2017/07/05/improving-data-science-ethics/ (accessed August 2019).

Frean, Alexandra (28 February 2018) "Britain has set the bar for EU data protection. We can't drop out now".

Frontier Economics (24 January 2017) "The UK Digital Sectors After Brexit", an independent report commissioned by techUK.

FTC – Privacy Shield, available at website https://www.ftc.gov/tips-advice/business-center/privacy-and-security/privacy-shield (accessed July 2019).

Greenleaf, Graham (2017) "Questioning 'adequacy' (PtI) – Japan", Privacy Laws & Business International Report, 1, 6-11 UNSW Law Research Paper No. 18-1.

Greenleaf, Graham (30 January 2016) "International Data Protection Agreements after the GDPR and Schrems", Privacy Laws & Business International Report 12-15, UNSW Law

Research Paper No. 2016-29).

Harcourt, Alison (3 December 2018) "Distress signals: how Brexit affects the Digital Single Market", LSE Brexit blog. Available at https://blogs.lse.ac.uk/brexit/2018/12/03/distress-signals-how-brexit-affects-the-digital-single-market/ (accessed August 2019).

Harding, Luke (2016) "The Snowden Files: The inside story of the world's most wanted man", Vintage Books.

Heim, Peter (2014) "The Quest for Clarity on Data Protection and Security", *Network Security*, p.8.

High Court of Justice, Queen's Bench Division, Divisional Court (27 April 2018) Liberty v. Home Office, Lord Justice Singh, case no: CO/1052/2017, EWHC 975 (Admin), London.

HM Government, Department for Digital, Culture, Media & Sports (23 April 2019) "No-deal Guidance: Amendments to UK data protection law in the event the UK leaves the EU without a deal". Available at https://www.gov.uk/government/publications/data-protection-law-eu-exit/amendments-to-uk-data-protection-law-in-the-event-the-uk-leaves-the-eu-without-a-deal-on-29-march-2019 (accessed April 2019).

HM Government, Department for Digital, Culture, Media & Sport; Department for Business; Energy & Industrial Strategy; and Information Commissioner's Office (6 February 2019) "Guidance: Using personal data after Brexit; When the UK leaves the EU there may be changes to the rules governing the use of personal data". Available at https://www.gov.uk/guidance/using-personal-data-after-brexit (accessed May 2019).

HM Government and Council of the European Union (25 November 2018) "Agreement on the withdrawal of the United Kingdom of Great Britain and Northern Ireland from the European Union and the European Atomic Energy Community, as endorsed by leaders at a special meeting of the European Council on 25 November 2018". Available at https://www.gov.uk/government/publications/withdrawal-agreement-and-political-declaration (accessed November 2018).

HM Government, DExEU (Department for Exiting the European Union) (November 2018) "EU (Withdrawal) Bill – Factsheet 6: Charter of fundamental rights". Available at https://assets.publishing.service.gov.uk/government/uploads/system/uploads/attachment_data/file/714377/6.pdf (accessed March 2019).

HM Government and European Council of the European Union (25 November 2018) "Political Declaration setting out the framework for the future relationship between the United Kingdom and the European Union", Department for Exiting the

European Union, European Commission, XT 21095/18, BXT 111, CO EUR-REP 54, Brussels. Available at UK Government website at https://www.gov.uk/government/publications/withdrawal-agreement-and-political-declaration and European Commission website at https://ec.europa.eu/commission/publications/political-declaration-setting-out-framework-future-relationship-between-european-union-and-united-kingdom_en (accessed November 2018).

HM Government, Department for Digital, Culture, Media & Sport (13 September 2018) "Data protection if there's no Brexit deal", Guidance. Available at https://www.gov.uk/government/publications/data-protection-if-theres-no-brexit-deal/data-protection-if-theres-no-brexit-deal (accessed January 2019). Note: This guidance was withdrawn on 1 March 2019 and replaced with the "Guidance: Using personal data after Brexit" (6 February 2019).

HM Government, Department for Exiting the European Union (24 August 2018) "The exchange and protection of personal data: A future partnership paper". Available at https://assets.publishing.service.gov.uk/government/uploads/system/uploads/attachment_data/file/639853/The_exchange_and_protection_of_personal_data.pdf (accessed April 2019).

HM Government, DExEU (7 June 2018) "Technical note: Benefits of a new data protection agreement." Available at https://assets.publishing.service.gov.uk/government/uploads/system/uploads/attachment_data/file/714677/Data_Protection_Technical_Note.pdf (accessed October 2018).

HM Government, Department of DCMS (13 June 2018) "Data Science Ethical Framework". Available at https://www.gov.uk/government/publications/data-ethics-framework (accessed August 2019).

HM Government, Home Office, Department for Digital, Culture, Media and Sport (25 May 2018) "Data Protection Act 2018: Factsheet – Intelligence services processing (Sections 82 – 113)". Available at https://assets.publishing.service.gov.uk/government/uploads/system/uploads/attachment_data/file/711233/2018-05-23_Factsheet_4_-_intelligence_services_processing.pdf (accessed February 2019).

HM Government, Department for Digital, Culture, Media & Sport (23 May 2018) "Data Protection Act 2018: Factsheet - Overview".

HM Government (May 2018) "Framework for the UK-EU partnership – Data Protection", presentation prepared by the UK negotiating team.

HM Government (18 September 2017) "Security, law enforcement and criminal justice: A future partnership paper".

HM Government, Government Digital Services (19 May 2016) "Data Science Ethical Framework (withdrawn on 13 June 2018). Available at https://www.gov.uk/government/publications/data-science-ethical-framework (accessed August 2019).

HM Government, European Union Committee (18 July 2017) "Brexit: The EU data protection package" 3rd Report of Session 2017-19, HL Paper 7.

House of Commons, European Scrutiny Committee (12 December 2018), Forty-eighth Report of Session 2017–19, HC 301-xlvii "[Document] 31 Personal data and the Council of Europe Convention". Available at https://publications.parliament.uk/pa/cm201719/cmselect/cmeuleg/301-xxxvii/30134.htm (accessed May 2019).

House of Commons, Homes Affairs Committee (9 October 2018) "UK-EU security cooperation after Brexit: Follow-up report: Government Response to the Committee's Seventh Report of Session 2017–19", Tenth Special Report of Session 2017–19.

House of Commons, Exiting the European Union Select Committee (3 July 2018) "The progress of the UK's negotiations on EU withdrawal: Data", Seventh Report of Session 2017–19, report together with formal minutes relating to the report, HC 1317.

House of Commons, Exiting the European Union Committee (26 June 2018) "The progress of the UK's negotiations on EU withdrawal: Data", Seventh Report of Session 2017-19, HC 1317. Available at https://www.parliament.uk/business/committees/committees-a-z/commons-select/exiting-the-european-union-committee/news-parliament-2017/progress-negotiations-data-report-published-17-19/ (accessed May 2019).

House of Commons Library (21 June 2017) "Brexit: red lines and principles", Briefing paper by Vaughne Miller, number 7938.

House of Lords, European Union Committee (11 July 2018) "Brexit: the proposed UK-EU security treaty", 18th Report of Session 2017-19.

House of Lords, Select Committee on Artificial Intelligence (16 April 2018) "Report of Session 2017-19 – AI in the UK: ready, willing and able?".

House of Lords, European Union Committee (18 July 2017) "Brexit: the EU data protection package", 3rd Report of Session 2017-19, HL Paper 7 Available at https://publications.parliament.uk/pa/ld201719/ldselect/ldeucom/7/702.htm (accessed February 2019).

House of Lords, European Union Committee (22 March 2017) "Brexit: trade in non-financial services", Chapter 5 Digital Services in the UK, 18th Report of Session 2016-17, HL Paper 135.

House of Lords (December 2016) "Brexit: future UK-EU security and police cooperation", report.

Human Rights Watch (30 June 2017) "Joint Letter to Five Eyes Intelligence Agencies Regarding Encryption". Available at https://www.hrw.org/news/2017/06/30/joint-letter-five-eyes-intelligence-agencies-regarding-encryption (accessed February 2019).

ICO blog – "Blog: How will personal data continue to flow after Brexit?". Available at https://ico.org.uk/about-the-ico/news-and-events/blog-how-will-personal-data-continue-to-flow-after-brexit/ (accessed February 2019).

ICO blog – "Blog: Data protection and Brexit - ICO advice for organisations", Information Commissioner Elizabeth Denham sets out how the ICO is helping businesses, particularly SMEs, prepare for a possible no-deal Brexit. Available at https://ico.org.uk/about-the-ico/news-and-events/blog-data-protection-and-brexit-ico-advice-for-organisations (accessed May 2019).

ICO – "Information rights and Brexit FAQs". Available at https://ico.org.uk/for-organisations/data-protection-and-brexit/information-rights-and-brexit-frequently-asked-questions/ (accessed June 2019).

ICO – "International transfers". Available at https://ico.org.uk/for-organisations/guide-to-data-protection/guide-to-the-general-data-protection-regulation-gdpr/international-transfers (accessed February 2019).

ICO – "Data protection and Brexit: Guidance and resources for organisations after Brexit". Available at https://ico.org.uk/for-organisations/data-protection-and-brexit/ (accessed June 2019)).

ICO – "Binding corporate rules". Available at https://ico.org.uk/for-organisations/binding-corporate-rules/ (accessed May 2019)).

ICO – "Certification". Available at https://ico.org.uk/for-organisations/guide-to-data-protection/guide-to-the-general-data-protection-regulation-gdpr/accountability-and-governance/certification/ (accessed June 2019).

ICO – "Codes of conduct". Available at https://ico.org.uk/for-organisations/guide-to-data-protection/guide-to-the-general-data-protection-regulation-gdpr/accountability-and-governance/codes-of-conduct/ (accessed June 2019).

ICO (March 2019) "Leaving the EU – six steps to take", v2.2.

Ismail, Noriswadi (2013) "Acclaiming Accountability: Preaching Best Practice" in Ismail, Noriswadi and Edwin Lee Yong Cieh (eds.) *Beyond Data Protection: Strategic Case Studies and Practical Guidance* (Springer).

International Chamber of Commerce (ICC) (23 January 2012) "ICC Data Protection Principles of Accountability Discussion Paper", ICC Commission on the Digital Economy, document No. 373/508 (Paris). Available at https://iccwbo.org/publication/icc-discussion-paper-on-data-protection-principle-of-accountability/ (accessed August 2019).

International Law Commission, United Nations "Analytical Guide to the Work of the International Law Commission" (Geneva). Available at http://legal.un.org/ilc/guide/11_1.shtml (accessed August 2019).

Khan, Mehreen (26 Feb 2019) "UK faces long wait for post-Brexit data deal, warns EU", *FT.com*.

Kostaki, Irene (27 February 2019) "EU's Data Protection Supervisor warns post-Brexit agreement could 'take years'", *New Europe*.

Kuner, Christopher (2017) "Reality and Illusion in EU Data Transfer Regulation Post Schrems", *German Law Journal* 881.

Kuner, Christopher (2013) Transborder Data Flows and Data Privacy Law (Oxford University Press, Oxford).

Kuner, Christopher (1 March 2011) "Table of Data Protection and Privacy Law Instruments Regulating Transborder Data Flows", Annex to the study "Regulation of Transborder Data Flows under Data Protection and Privacy Law: Past, Present, and Future" (Tilburg University).

Kuner, Christopher (2010) "Regulation of Transborder Data Flows Under Data Protection and Privacy Law: Past, Present, and Future", TILT Law & Technology Working Paper No. 016/2010.

Kuner, Christopher (2009a) "An International Legal Framework for Data Protection: Issues and Prospects", *Computer Law & Security Review*, Vol. 25, pp. 307-317.

Kuner, Christopher (2009b) "Developing an Adequate Legal Framework for International Data Transfers", in Gutwirth (ed.) *Reinventing Data Protection?* pp. 263-273. (Springer Science + Business Media B.V.)

Lambert, Paul (2018) Understanding the New European Data Protection Rules, Taylor & Francis Group.

Lawson, Laurence Sean (18 October 2018) "What will be the future of data flows between the EU and the UK post-Brexit?" MICL Thesis, Faculty of Law, Univ. of Helsinki. Available at https://helda.helsinki.fi/bitstream/handle/10138/277847/Lawson_Laurence_pro_gradu_2018.pdf (accessed August 2019).

Lee, Phil (20 September 2018) "Every vendor wants to be... a data controller?!", *fieldfisher – Privacy, Security and Information Law*. Available at https://privacylawblog.fieldfisher.com/2018/every-vendor-wants-to-be-a-data-controller (accessed August 2019).

Liberty (11 June 2019) "MI5 'unlawfully' handled bulk surveillance data, liberty litigation reveals". Available at https://www.libertyhumanrights.org.uk/news/press-releases-and-statements/mi5-"unlawfully"-handled-bulk-surveillance-data-liberty (accessed May 2019).

Liberty (29 November 2018) "Liberty wins the right to challenge bulk surveillance under snoopers' charter". Available at https://www.libertyhumanrights.org.uk/news/press-releases-and-statements/liberty-wins-right-challenge-bulk-surveillance-under-snoopers' (accessed May 2019).

Liberty (13 September 2018) "Human rights organisations win landmark battle against UK mass surveillance". Available at https://www.libertyhumanrights.org.uk/news/press-releases-and-statements/human-rights-organisations-win-landmark-battle-against-uk-mass (accessed May 2019).

Liberty (27 April 2018) "Liberty wins first battle in landmark challenge to mass surveillance powers in the Investigatory Powers Act". Available at https://www.libertyhumanrights.org.uk/news/press-releases-and-statements/liberty-wins-first-battle-landmark-challenge-mass-surveillance (accessed May 2019).

MacAskill, Ewen; Hopkins, Nick; Davies, Nick and Ball, James (21 June 2013) "How does GCHQ's internet surveillance work", *The Guardian*. Available at https://www.theguardian.com/uk/2013/jun/21/how-does-gchq-internet-surveillance-work (accessed August 2019).

McGoogan, Cara (13 March 2017) "UK watchdog to hire hundreds as it prepares for country to adopt a 'once in a generation' crackdown on data misuse". Available at https://www.telegraph.co.uk/technology/2017/03/12/uk-watchdog-hire-hundreds-data-crackdown/ (accessed January 2019).

Meunier, Sophie and Kalypso Nicolaidis (6 September 2006) "The European Union as a conflicted trade power", *Journal of European Public Policy*, 13:6, pp. 906-925 (Routledge: Taylor & Francis Group).

Milanovic, Marko (March 2014) "Human Rights Treaties and Foreign Surveillance: Privacy in the Digital Age", *Harvard international Law Journal* 56 (1). pp. 81-146.

Newscabal (11 August 2018) "Companies review arrangements for data transfer after Brexit".

Nixon, Simon (29 June 2017) "Britain cannot simply walk away from the European Court of Justice", *The Times*, London.

OECD (2013) "The OECD Privacy Framework: Guidelines Governing the Protection of Privacy and Transborder Flows of Personal Data ("Privacy Guidelines"), revised recommendations, OECD Working Party on Information Security and Privacy. Available at http://oecd.org/sti/ieconomy/oecd_privacy_framework.pdf (accessed July 2019).

Osbourne, Samuel (18 May 2017) "Conservative manifesto: Theresa May announces UK will remain part of European Convention of Human Rights", *The Independent*. Available at https://www.independent.co.uk/news/uk/politics/conservative-manifesto-uk-echr-european-convention-human-rights-leave-eu-next-parliament-election-a7742436.html (accessed August 2019).

Price, Ian (15 Sep 2017) "Laws on data protection must be a Brexit priority", *Western Mail*, Cardiff.

Prime Minister Theresa May (17 February 2018) "PM speech at Munich Security Conference", speech transcript. Available at https://www.gov.uk/government/speeches/pm-speech-at-munich-security-conference-17-february-2018 (accessed June 2019).

Prime Minister Theresa May (22 September 2017) "PM's Florence speech: a new era of cooperation and partnership between the UK and the EU", speech transcript. Available at https://www.gov.uk/government/speeches/pms-florence-speech-a-new-era-of-cooperation-and-partnership-between-the-uk-and-the-eu (accessed June 2019).

Privacy Shield Framework website "Privacy Shield and the UK FAQs" at https://www.privacyshield.gov/article?id=Privacy-Shield-and-the-UK-FAQs (accessed June 2019).

Proust, Oliver (18 February 2019) "EDPB prepares for a 'no deal' Brexit", *fieldfisher – Privacy, Security and Information Law*. Available at https://privacylawblog.fieldfisher.com/2019/edpb-prepares-for-a-no-deal-brexit (accessed August 2019).

Ram, Aliya; Megaw, Nicholas; Khan, Mehreen (11 August 2018a) "Companies review arrangements for data transfer after Brexit", *FT.com*, London/Brussels.

Ram, Aliya; Megaw, Nicholas; Khan, Mehreen (11 August 2018b) "Data snags loom in event of no-deal Brexit", Financial Times, London, p18.) (Ram, Aliya; Megaw, Nicholas; Khan, Mehreen (11 Aug 2018) "Companies review arrangements for data transfer after Brexit", *FT.com*.

Royal Court of Justice Judgement (27 April 2018) The Queen on the application of The National Council for Liberties (Liberty) vs (1) Secretary of State for the Home Department and (2) Secretary of State for Foreign and Commonwealth Affairs "Justice v. Home Office [2018]", case No: CO/1052/2017, EWHC 975 (Admin), London.

Sayer, Peter (7 August 2017) "Campaigners ask court to reveal extent of spying by Five Eyes Alliance", *Business Source Premier*.

Sheftalovich, Zoya (29 February 2016) "5 Takeaways from the Privacy Shield", *POLITICO*.

Stone, Jon (23 Aug 2017) "British data protection laws to stay 'aligned' with the EU's after Brexit", *The Independent* (Online), Independent Digital News & Media, London.

Sunday Independent (25 March 2018) "Will the UK still be a safe place for your data post-Brexit?", Dublin.

Surveillance Camera Commissioner (January 2019) "Annual Report 2017/18", presented to parliament pursuant to Section 35(1)(b) of the Protection of Freedoms Act 2012.

techUK *et al* (November 2017) "No Interruptions: options for the future UK-EU data sharing relationship", a joint report commissioned from international law firm Dentons, techUK and UK Finance.

Telegraph (18 June 2018) "EU could cancel Brexit security deal if UK quits European Court of Human Rights", *Telegraph.co.uk*, London.

Telegraph (23 May 2018) "Britain to follow EU data rules in full after Brexit in bid to save trade ties", *Telegraph.co.uk*, London.

The Court (Grand Chamber) Judgement (6 October 2015) *Maximillian Schrems v Data Protection Commissioner (Ireland)*, case C-362/14, preliminary ruling from the High Court (Ireland)).

Thompson, Barney and Parker, George (24 August 2017) "UK seeks bespoke deal with EU on data protection", *FT.com*.

Trentmann, Nina (12 Mar 2019) "Companies Weigh Data-Privacy Risks Ahead of Brexit; A no-deal breakup between the U.K. and the EU could lead to a compliance gap with the bloc's data-protection laws", *Wall Street Journal* (Online), New York.

United Nations Conference on Trade and Development (UNCTAD) (2016), United Nations "Data protection regulations and international data flows: Implications for trade and development" (Geneva). Available at https://unctad.org/en/PublicationsLibrary/dtlstict2016d1_en.pdf (accessed July 2019).

US Congress Judicial Redress Act of 2015 (Public Law No. 114-126 (02/24/2016), 5 USC §552.

United Nations (14 December 1990) "Guidelines for the Regulation of Computerized Personal Data Files", adopted by General Assembly resolution 45/95.

Vanberg, Aysem Diker and Maelya Maunick (2018) "Data protection in the UK post-Brexit: the only certainty is uncertainty", *International Review of Law, Computers & Technology*, Volume 32, Issue 1, 190-206. Available at website https://www.tandfonline.com/doi/abs/10.1080/13600869.2018.1434754 (accessed August 2019).

Weber, Rolf H. and Dominic Staiger (2017) "Transatlantic Data Protection in Practice", Centre for Information Technology, Society and Law (Springer).

Worley, Will (29 December 2016) "Theresa May will 'campaign to leave the European Convention on Human Rights in the 2020 election'", *The Independent*. Available at https://www.independent.co.uk/news/uk/politics/theresa-may-campaign-leave-european-convention-on-human-rights-2020-general-election-brexit-a7499951.html (accessed August 2019).

Other publications on topics and trends in the industry available on Amazon and extended distribution channels include the following –

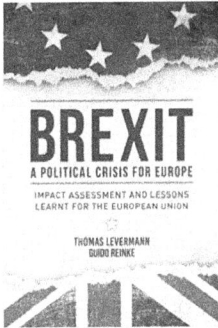

This book offers the first comprehensive impact assessment across the 35 *acquis* EU policy domains. The assessment ranges from the four freedoms of the Single Market – free movement of goods, services, capital and person – to essential matter like companies and competition, financial services, information society, consumer protection, energy, science & research, employment, security & defence, and more. It also provides background information and a vision of Britain and the EU in 2026.

Brexit: A Political Crisis for Europe: Impact Assessment and Lessons Learnt for the European Union (GOLD RUSH Publishing, London). ISBN-10: 1908585099.

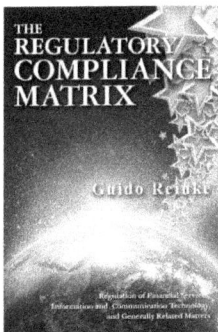

This book with more than 2500 entries brings clarity to a domain which is widely considered to be complex, unstructured, and in constant flux. It is a compendious guide to the laws, regulations, standards, and recommendations applicable to compliance programmes. The Regulatory Compliance Matrix has been a bestseller in the category business law on Amazon for several months.

The Regulatory Compliance Matrix: Regulation of Financial Services, Information and Communication Technology, and Generally Related Matters (GOLD RUSH Publishing, London). ISBN-10: 1908585056.

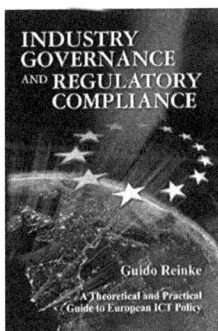

This book contains detailed guidance on how to participate in the making and comply with the output of regulatory regimes. It provides evidence for the Industry Governance Theory, which is a new take on regulatory governance that gives insight into industry's pro-active role and predominating influence in shaping European public policy. The book also introduces new tools such the Regulatory Compliance Maturity Model, the Policy Influence-Timing Model and the Stakeholder Action Matrix.

Industry Governance and Regulatory Compliance: A Theoretical and Practical Guide to European ICT Policy (GOLD RUSH Publishing, London). ISBN-10: 1908585021.

SOME FINAL PRIVACY THOUGHS BY CELEBRITIES

I have as much privacy as a goldfish in a bowl.

Princess Margaret Rose Windsor, Countess of Snowdon

I don't want to write an autobiography because I would become
public property with no privacy left.

Stephen Hawking, English theoretical physicist, cosmologist and author

Privacy means people know what they're signing up for, in plain English, and
repeatedly.
I'm an optimist, I believe people are smart, and
some people want to share more than other people do.
Ask them. Ask them every time.
Make them tell you to stop asking them if they get tired of your asking them.
Let them know precisely what you're going to do with their data.

Steve Jobs; American business magnate, entrepreneur and co-founder of Apple

Privacy is dead,
and social medial holds the smoking gun.

Pete Cashmore, founder and CEO of Mashable

Relying on the government to protect your privacy
is like asking a peeping Tom to install your window blinds.

John Perry Barlow, American poet and essayist

Privacy is not something that I'm merely entitled to,
it's a absolute prerequisite.

Marlo Brando, American actor and film director

Getting information from the Internet
is like
taking a drink from a hydrant.

Mitchell Kapor, founder of Lotus Development Corporation

www.ingramcontent.com/pod-product-compliance
Lightning Source LLC
Chambersburg PA
CBHW051414200326
41520CB00023B/7237